**Your Money:
Frustration
or Freedom?**

D0632941

YOUR MONEY:
FRUSTRATION OR FREEDOM

HOWARD L. DAYTON, JR.

 Tyndale House
Publishers, Inc.
Wheaton, Illinois

Scripture quotations, unless otherwise identified, are from
The Living Bible, Copyright © 1971 by
Tyndale House Publishers,
Wheaton, Ill.

Fourth printing, April 1982

Library of Congress Catalog Card Number 78-68805
ISBN 0-8423-8725-0 paper.
Copyright © 1979 by Howard L. Dayton, Jr.
Printed in the United States of America.

To Bev,
my wife,
God's choice gift
to our family

To Matthew,
my beloved son

To Jim Seneff,
for without his vision
and effort,
this book would never
have been conceived

To Will Norton, Jr.,
for without his skill
and encouragement,
this book would never
have been born

CONTENTS

ONE
THE PROBLEM

When I was young, I used to think that money was the most important thing in life; now that I am older, I know it is.

Oscar Wilde

Allen and Jean Hitchcock decided to end their marriage of twenty-four years.

In anticipation of the divorce settlement, Allen began to review the family's financial records. As he sorted through the files, he came across an old faded check made out to the hotel where he and Jean had stayed on their honeymoon. Another check had paid for an installment on their first car. He picked up still another check and remembered with fatherly pride how he had made it out to the hospital when their daughter was born. And then there was that $1,500 down payment on their first home . . . .

After several hours of sorting through such checks, Allen realized how much he and his wife had invested in their marriage. He paused, deep in thought for several minutes. Then he closed the file and dialed his wife's number. After an awkward exchange he blurted out the reason for his call. Would she work with him to rebuild their marriage?

While a family crisis such as Allen's and Jean's may be foreign to some of us, the message of their family's checks is common. It is the story of our lives. It tells of our values, how much we save, what we spend, to whom we give. In fact, our checkbooks tell us more about our priorities than does anything else.

That's why Jesus talked so much about money. Sixteen of the thirty-eight parables were concerned with how to handle money and possessions. Indeed, Howard Hendricks notes that "Jesus Christ said more about money than [about] heaven or hell combined." In the Gospels an amazing one out of ten verses (288 in all) deal directly with the subject of money. The Bible offers 500 verses on prayer, less than 500 verses on faith, but more than 2,000 verses on money and possessions.

The Lord must have realized that managing money and possessions would be a problem for most people. He said a lot about it because he wants us to know his perspective concerning this critical area of life.

Clearly, he considered money and possessions important. He dealt with money matters because money matters.

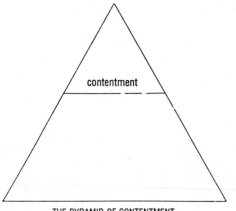

THE PYRAMID OF CONTENTMENT

TWO
THE ANSWER

The Bible is the blueprint for living.

I was sliding papers and reports into my briefcase when the phone rang on my desk. It was 5:30 P.M., and I was getting ready to go home after a long day of paperwork and personal conferences. I was tired and irritated. Reluctantly, I picked up the phone.

"Hello, Howard. This is Allen Hitchcock."

I felt a pang of embarrassment. I had neglected to return his earlier call. He sounded depressed, and I made a lame apology for not calling him back.

"Jean and I considered a divorce, but decided to try to work it out," he said, his voice sounding strained.

Their financial problems were on the verge of destroying their marriage. They turned to me. We had become acquainted at church two years before when they had moved from St. Louis.

Allen earned $17,400 a year as a purchasing agent for a major grocery chain in Orlando. He couldn't understand where the money went. And he and Jean didn't foresee a brighter future. The family faced increasing expenses to keep up with inflation and to pay for dental work, music lessons, and other items to which they had become accustomed. Then in a few years there would be college expenses for the four children.

In addition, the Hitchcocks owed almost $9,000 to retail stores, doctors, credit card companies, and finance companies. Moreover, they owed $37,500 on their home mortgage.

Because of their debts and their increasing daily expenses, the Hitchcocks shopped carefully, sometimes checking half a dozen outlets for the best price. They bought the best quality merchandise and saved cents-off coupons for the supermarkets. To try to save additional costs, Allen did most of the automobile repairs and Jean avoided buying expensive convenience foods.

But the family faced a critical problem. Jean and Allen never had been able to budget their spending. They seldom made the decision not to buy what they wanted. They just did not have clear guidelines for handling their money and possessions.

I understood their frustrations. Several years before, a friend, Jim Seneff, and I found ourselves making daily financial decisions without a Scriptural point of reference for our expanding businesses and young families.

We had been taught a lot about what the Bible says concerning sharing and giving, but nothing on how to handle the rest of our money. We felt that to be the best husbands and the best businessmen we could be, we had to do a thorough study of what Scripture said about money.

Together we read the entire Bible, locating each verse that dealt with money and arranging those verses by topics. We shared this with a number of close friends. The enthusiastic response encouraged us to put this information into a more communicable format and share it with our church. Their excitement was startling. They bombarded us with questions and described to us several areas of intense frustration. Gradually this study developed into a full-fledged seminar that is today conducted in churches throughout the nation.

From the comments of those who have attended the seminar, it is apparent that the Hitchcocks are not an isolated case. Indeed, financial predicaments such as the

Hitchcocks' are not limited to our country. This is a worldwide problem.

WORLD ECONOMIC PROBLEMS

Great shifts in the world's economy have occurred in the last decade—shifts which could lead to a disintegrating global economy. The tremors which began in the 1960s have led to major rumblings in the 1970s and threaten to erupt during the 1980s.

Unprecedented conditions have caused many respected experts in the economic fraternity to predict global financial chaos. Almost every month a new book hits the bookstores describing an imminent "depression," "collapse," or "crash." Frankly, given the direction of the world economy, it is easy to see why so many professionals have painted such a gloomy picture.

The 1970s have been economically traumatic. It has been a decade of the first global, double-digit inflation during peacetime and the highest number of unemployed since the Great Depression. Early in the decade the Arab petroleum-exporting nations formed a cartel, then hit the world with an embargo on the world's basic source of energy—oil—followed by a 400 percent increase in oil prices. This has meant higher prices around the world for just about everything.

AMERICAN ECONOMIC PROBLEMS

Closer to home, America also has major unsolved problems. The U. S. Treasury keeps piling one huge deficit on another. The end of the flow of red ink is nowhere in sight. In fact, interest alone on the federal debt now exceeds the entire federal budget of 1950.

Since 1967 prices have jumped more than 100 percent. For example, a combination of goods and services that cost $100 ten years ago would be more than $200 today. That's inflation—loss of purchasing power.

If prices keep climbing at 6 percent a year, a dollar that buys 100 cents' worth of goods today will buy only 75 cents' worth five years from now and 56 cents' worth in 1988.

THE FAMILY

The effort to keep up with inflation is a struggle for the American family. Although wages have been increasing, according to the U. S. Department of Labor the average family of four actually has *lost* purchasing power since 1973 because of inflation and higher taxes.

HOW INFLATION GOBBLES UP YOUR PAYCHECK

Average Family of Four

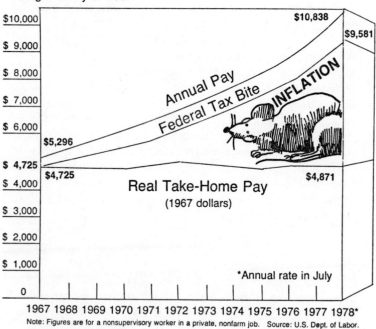

Note: Figures are for a nonsupervisory worker in a private, nonfarm job.   Source: U.S. Dept. of Labor.

To try to cope, 72 percent of Americans have made some changes in their style of living, according to a recent *New York Times*-CBS News poll.

The changes have been painful. "I don't think people making my salary used to worry like we do now," reflected Daniel Peters, a communications manager in

Chicago. He earns about $30,000 a year. Coping with inflation can produce enormous emotional strains, too. One couple described their feelings as "a constant state of anxiety." "We have a feeling of desperation," the wife said.

The problems facing American families today seem insurmountable. For the first time Americans are feeling that they cannot enjoy the "good life." Look at housing for instance.

The American dream house has passed $50,000. It is evident that the single-family house is becoming unattainable for millions of middle-income families who traditionally have considered a house to be part of the American birthright. Housing experts predict that by 1990 only 25 percent of Americans will be able to own their own homes.

For people who do not want to reduce their standard of living, the loss of purchasing power caused by inflation must be made up in other ways.

The most common way has been for people to spend more than they earn, then borrow to make up the difference. In fact, the average American family spends $400 a year more than it earns. Debt in the United States increases at more than $1,000 a second.

These statistics indicate that the American family is facing an unprecedented financial crisis. A recent survey showed that more than 50 percent of all divorces are caused by financial pressures in the home. For many, the better marriage vow would have been "till debt do us part!"

THE ANSWER

Increasingly, Americans wonder where they can turn for help. There are two basic alternatives—society and the Bible. Historically American society, especially in our rural economy, taught people to work hard, develop skills, be thrifty, avoid debt, and save. Many of these practices stemmed from the Bible. However, the last several decades have seen a dramatic shift in our culture's values and practices in handling money. Today society's answers are in striking contradiction to the Bible. To help the reader recognize the contradictions, a brief comparison appears at the end of each chapter under the heading "Contrast." Nowhere is this contradiction more apparent than in the perspective of how money relates to our personal goals.

Psychologists tell us that personal peace and prosperity is the goal of most people in our society. Modern thinking associates achievement of this goal with how much we have acquired. Only as we accumulate enough assets to satisfy our particular lifestyle are we supposed to experience personal peace and fulfillment.

But such a perspective of money conflicts with Scripture. The Bible teaches that we can learn to be content in any circumstance—in poverty as well as prosperity.

Not that I was ever in need, for I have learned how to get along happily whether I have much or little. I know how to live on almost nothing or with everything. I have learned the secret of contentment in every situation, whether it be a full stomach or hunger, plenty or want.

Philippians 4:11, 12

The purpose of this book is to teach you the biblical principles of handling money and possessions. The book is designed to give you practical ways of integrating these principles into your life. As you learn the principles and practice them, the result will be contentment.

Each chapter of this book relates to a specific principle. To help you understand how each principle contributes to contentment, a pyramid will be used as a guide. At the pinnacle of the pyramid is contentment. Each chapter will then be a building block in the pyramid leading to that pinnacle. When all the chapters are completed and the blocks in place, you will know and be equipped to experience the secret of contentment. Use the progression of the pyramid throughout the book to put your own financial life in order.

CONTRAST

Society says: You will find happiness and peace as you accumulate enough wealth to support your desired standard of living.

Scripture says: As you learn and follow the scriptural principles of how to handle your money and possessions, you can be content in every circumstance.

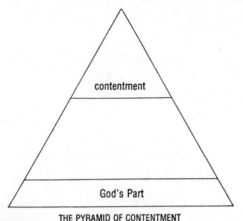

THE PYRAMID OF CONTENTMENT

THREE
GOD'S PART—
THE FOUNDATION

Yours is the mighty power and glory and victory and majesty. Everything in the heavens and earth is yours, O Lord, and this is your kingdom. We adore you as being in control of everything. Riches and honor come from you alone, and you are the ruler of all mankind; your hand controls power and might, and it is at your discretion that men are made great and given strength.

King David, 1 Chronicles 29:11, 12

On a rainy November morning Allen and Jean Hitchcock arrived at my office to work through their financial problems and save their marriage.

Allen and Jean were Christians, but they had never been exposed to the Bible's perspective on money and possessions. They appreciated their beautiful two-story brick house in suburban Orlando, their two late-model automobiles, and their other possessions. Both felt that they had worked hard for what they had and that they had earned the right to enjoy their "peace and prosperity."

However, after financial pressures threatened their prosperity, their lack of peace surfaced in marital crisis. Allen realized that there was a serious lack of communications about the family finances. He and Jean each had their own hopes and opinions on how to spend the family income, but somehow they had never mentioned them to each other.

They were close to losing everything to their creditors. That, coupled with the possibility of divorce, had jarred them from their complacency. So when I sat down with Allen and Jean the Friday after Thanksgiving, they were motivated to learn what the Bible says about money.

Scripture teaches there are two distinct parts to the handling of our money and possessions: the part God plays and the part we play. I believe most of the confusion relating to the handling of money arises from the fact that these two parts are not clearly understood.

The Bible declares that the foundation of contentment is the part that the living God plays in our finances. Let's examine what the Bible has to say about God's part in three crucial areas: ownership, control, and provision.

OWNERSHIP

The Bible clearly states that God is sole owner of everything.

The earth belongs to God; everything in all the world is his! He is the one who pushed the oceans back to let dry land appear.

Psalm 24:1

. . . Everything in the heavens and earth is yours, O Lord, and this is your kingdom.

1 Chronicles 29:11

What God makes clear is that he created and owns the world. The Bible repeatedly reminds us of this. It even lists some of the specific items belonging to God. For example, he owns the land (Leviticus 25:23), all the animals on the earth (Psalm 50:10), and all the silver and gold (Haggai 2:8).

To learn to be content, you must recognize God as the owner of all your possessions. If you believe you own even a single possession, then the circumstances that affect that possession will be reflected in your attitude. If something favorable happens to that possession, then you will be happy; but if something bad occurs, you will be discontent.

Let me give you an illustration. After Jim Seneff went through the exercise of transferring to God ownership of everything he possessed, he bought a car to replace the automobile that he had been driving. When it was just two days old a young girl drove into the side of it. Jim's first reaction was, "Well, God, I don't know why you want a dent in the side of your new car, but you have one!"

Similarly, when John Wesley learned that his home had been destroyed by fire, he exclaimed, "The Lord's house burned. One less responsibility for me!"

Yet it's not easy to hold this perspective consistently. We find it too easy to think that the possessions we have and the money we earn are entirely the result of *our* skills and achievements, and that we have earned the right to their ownership. I am the master of my fate, the humanist says. I alone own my possessions. Obviously, this view of ownership is the heritage we receive from our culture.

In 1914 Harvey Calkins wrote *Elements of Stewardship*. In that book he contrasted the heritage we receive from our society with what the Bible teaches:

"There has been but one nation whose concept of property ownership was based on ownership by a personal God, and that nation was Israel. All the other nations we have knowledge of—the Egyptians, the Greeks, the Romans—their underlying philosophy of the ownership of property and their laws relating to property were based on the concept of the individual owning what he possessed.

"Where did we receive our standards of property ownership? It is rooted in the law of the Roman empire. The Roman philosophy of life, crystallized in Roman law and through that law standardized in Christian civilization, was not built on 'the law of the Lord—ownership by God'; it was based on the laws of man—ownership by man.

"The average man, unless he has met the issues squarely and jarred himself loose from inherited traditions, remains caught in a false concept of property ownership. His Christian instinct is entangled with the honest belief that he is the owner of what he has merely been given to possess. His whole history and entire culture compel him to believe that he is the owner of his property."

One of the most traumatic times Bev and I have had in our marriage was when our son, Matthew, was six months old and became seriously ill. His temperature skyrocketed to 105 degrees and he turned beet-red.

We rushed him to the emergency room at the hospital. While the doctor conducted tests for what he suspected was spinal meningitis, Bev and I wept over our dearest possession—our only child.

Only when we came to grips with the fact that our heavenly Father loves Matthew even more than we do, did we have the confidence to entrust him with ownership of our son. When Matthew recovered, we were grateful for his health and our lesson in ownership.

Giving up ownership is not easy, nor is it a once-and-for-all transaction. We constantly need to be reminded that God owns all our possessions.

CONTROL

The Old Testament gives special attention to the fact that God is in control of circumstances.

Examine several of the 272 names of God in Scripture: Master, Almighty, Creator, Shepherd, Lord of lords, King of kings. It's obvious who is in charge:

. . . We adore you as being in control of everything. Riches and honor come from you alone, and you are the Ruler of all mankind; your hand controls power and might, and it is at your discretion that men are made great and given strength.

1 Chronicles 29:11, 12

Daniel proclaims this in his prayer of praise after God reveals King Nebuchadnezzar's dream to him:

Blessed be the name of God forever and ever, for he alone has all wisdom and all power. World events are under his control. He removes kings and sets others on their thrones.
                                                          Daniel 2:20, 21

What a view for an eighteen-year-old man to have. This recognition of God's sovereign control of all circumstances continued with Daniel throughout his life. As he neared the age of eighty-five, he was condemned to the lions' den—although he was innocent before men and God. Despite his predicament, he was content.

In the book of Daniel he described the situation. He did not dwell on the seemingly hopeless circumstances of the cruel lions' den. Instead, Daniel focused on King Darius who appeared to have everything a man could want. He lived in the magnificent Babylonian palace—one of the seven wonders of the ancient world. As king, his word was law. He had all the wealth of the kingdom at his disposal. Nonetheless, he was not content: "Then the king returned to his palace and went to bed without dinner. He refused his usual entertainment and didn't sleep all night" (Daniel 6:18).

The contrast between these two men could not be more distinct: Daniel in terrible circumstances, but content; Darius in ideal circumstances, but discontent.

The difference in attitude between these two men was that Daniel recognized that God was in absolute control of all circumstances, no matter how impossible the solution seemed. Darius did not.

The message is obvious. You can experience contentment only when you recognize that God is in control of all the circumstances around you. This is difficult in extreme circumstances and even more difficult during the trivial situations that seem to hassle us every day.

For example, when I get caught in the morning traffic on Interstate 4 driving in to work, I have two options: I can get uptight and angry at the inconvenience of wasting "my time," or I can realize that God controls time and he has allowed me to get caught in traffic for a purpose.

God is the creator and controller of the universe; yet

he is also intimately involved in each of our lives.
Nowhere is this more evident than in his promises of
provision.

PROVISION

In Genesis 22:14, God is spoken of as "Jehovah-Jireh,"
which means "The Lord will provide." He takes care of his
people, and he does not need a booming economy to
provide for them.

*All mankind scratches for its daily bread, but your
heavenly Father knows your needs. He will always give you
all you need from day to day . . . .*
                                          Luke 12:30, 31

The Lord has promised to provide our needs. In
1 Timothy 6:8 he tells us what our needs are—food and
covering. In other words, there is a difference between
needs and wants. A need is a basic necessity of life—food,
clothing, or shelter. A want is anything more than a need.
A steak dinner, a new car, and the latest fashions—they
are all wants.
The Lord has obligated himself to provide our needs,
but he has not promised to provide our wants. This is the
heart of contentment—on one hand the Lord promises to
provide our needs, and on the other tells us to be content
when these needs are met. "And if we have food and
covering, with these we shall be content" (1 Timothy 6:8,
NASB).
Let me illustrate his provision with a story: "As World
War II was drawing to a close, the Allied armies gathered
up many hungry orphans. They were placed in camps
where they were well fed. Despite excellent care, they
slept poorly. They seemed nervous and afraid.
"Finally, a psychologist came up with a solution. Each
child was given a piece of bread to hold after he was put
to bed. If he was hungry, more food was provided but
when he was finished, this particular piece of bread was
just to be held—not eaten.
"The piece of bread produced wonderful results. The

children went to bed, instinctively knowing they would have food to eat the next day. That guarantee gave the children a restful and contented sleep."[1]

Similarly, the Lord has given us his guarantee—our "piece of bread." As we cling to his promises of provision, we can relax and be content. "And my God shall supply all your needs according to his riches" (Philippians 4:19, NASB).

So even if you are in the middle of an extreme financial problem, you can be content because the Lord has promised to feed, clothe, and shelter you.

Stop! Think about what God's part really is: He is the owner, he is in sovereign control of every circumstance, and he has promised to meet our needs. The God who created the world and holds it together is a powerful God. He is able to perform his responsibilities and keep his promises. Reflect on that for a moment.

God's part is only one-half of the equation. It is the most important part, but it is only half. In the next chapter we will examine the other half, our part.

CONTRAST

Society says: What I possess I alone own, and I alone control my destiny.

Scripture says: What I possess, God owns. He is the sovereign, living God who controls all events.

At the end of most chapters, after the CONTRAST between society and Scripture, there will be a COMMITMENT section that will give you the opportunity to practice the biblical principle we have just covered. I challenge and encourage you to do the COMMITMENT sections because they will help make the principles a part of your life.

COMMITMENT

In our seminars we go through an exercise of transferring the ownership of our possessions to the Lord. We use a deed to do this because a deed is often used to transfer the ownership of property.

When participants in our seminar complete and sign the deed, they are giving up ownership of "their possessions" and are acknowledging that God is owner of their assets.

The exercise is important because we all occasionally forget that God owns everything. We act as if we own it. By signing the deed, a person establishes a specific time when God's ownership is acknowledged. Thus, a person can repeatedly refer to the document and recall that God owns everything.

The following will help you complete the deed:

1) Print your name. You are the grantor, the one transferring ownership.

2) Write your home address.

3) We have already printed, "The Lord our God" (he is the one receiving the assets).

4) Write *contentment*. That is what we receive for transferring the property to the Lord.

5) Give prayerful consideration to those possessions which you wish to acknowledge God owns. Then list these items.

6) Sign your name.

7) On the lower right-hand corner there is a space for the signature of two witnesses. These friends can help hold you accountable in a practical way for recognizing God as owner of your possessions.

DEED

This Deed *Made the   day of   A. D. 19*

by _____

hereinafter called the grantor,
whose address is
to the grantee: The Lord Our God

Witnesseth: *That the grantor, for and*
in consideration of
and other valuable considerations, receipt whereof is
hereby acknowledged, hereby releases, conveys and
confirms unto the grantee, all that certain

In Witness Whereof, *the said*
grantor has hereunto set   hand and seal
the day and year first above written.

Signed, sealed and delivered in our presence:

To Have and to Hold, *the same in*
fee simple forever.

_____

_____

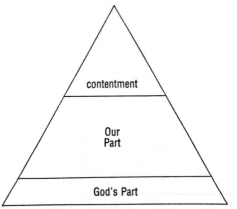

THE PYRAMID OF CONTENTMENT

FOUR
OUR PART—
GOOD AND FAITHFUL

Well done, good and faithful servant; you have been faithful over a little, I will set you over much; enter into the joy of your master.

Matthew 25:21, RSV

Contentment is the product of the faithful discharge of our duties.

After he and Jean finished signing the deed, Allen slid it across the desk.

"I feel a lot of relief," he said. "But I also feel like I'm supposed to do something." And Allen was right.

We cannot just sit back, do nothing, and wait for God to perform. We have a responsibility. But, like Allen, we may not know exactly what our part is. To help us out, let's compare some of the names God gives himself with the names God gives man:

God	*Man*
Shepherd	*Sheep*
Father	*Children*
Eternal	*Vapor*
Creator	*Dust*

Vine	*Branches*
Head	*Body*
Master	*Steward*

All of these names either compare or describe a facet of God's relationship with man. When it comes to financial concerns, the words *master* and *steward* most precisely describe the relationship of God to man in a way that reflects our respective responsibilities.

God, the Master, is the owner of everything, the controller of all events, and our provider. Man's part is to be a steward. Now the word *steward* can be translated into three different words: *manager, supervisor,* and *overseer.* In Scripture the position of a steward is one of great responsibility. He is the supreme authority under his master and has full responsibility for all his master's possessions, household affairs, and raising of children.

As we examine Scripture we see that God, as Master, has given man the authority to be steward.

You [God] have put him [man] in charge of everything you made; everything is put under his authority.

Psalm 8:6

Man's only responsibility is to be faithful.

Moreover it is required in stewards, that a man be found faithful.

1 Corinthians 4:2, KJV

As Christians we have been taught much about giving, but little about how to faithfully handle all our money. However, God is not only concerned with the amount we give, but also with what we do with our entire income. In fact, he is interested in all that we have. By giving a small percentage, many Christians feel that they can bypass all other responsibilities and do as they please with the remainder of their money.

The issue in Scripture is how to handle faithfully all God has entrusted to us. The faithful steward is responsible for what he has, whether he has much or little. He can be wasteful and negligent whether he is poor or wealthy. In the 25th chapter of Matthew, God required good stewardship of the man who was given two talents as well as the man who was given five.

FAITHFULNESS

I believe God requires us to faithfully use our possessions for three reasons: 1) to develop character; 2) to deepen spiritual life; 3) and to lead us to contentment.

The Faithful Use of Money Develops Character.   David McConaughy authored a book, *Money the Acid Test*, around the turn of the century. In it he said, "Money, most common of temporal things, involves uncommon and eternal consequences. Even though it may be done quite unconsciously, money molds men—in the process of getting it, of saving it, of using it, of giving it, of accounting for it. Depending upon how it is handled, it proves a blessing or a curse to its possessor; either the man becomes master of his money, or the money becomes master of the man. It has more magical qualities than Aladdin's lamp. Depending upon whether he is a faithful steward or not, he becomes:

In acquiring, either a benefactor or an extractor;
In spending, a provider or a prodigal;
In saving, a conserver or a miser;
In giving, a philanthropist or a patronizer;
In accounting, a creditor or a debtor;
In influencing others, a stepping stone or a stumbling block.

"Our Lord takes money, the thing that, essential though it is to our common life, sometimes seems so sordid, and he makes it a touchstone to test the lives of men and an instrument for molding them into the likeness of himself."[2]

Clearly, if we are handling our possessions as faithful stewards, our character is being built. If we are unfaithful, our character is being torn down.

Perhaps Richard Halverson said it most precisely:

"Jesus Christ said more about money than any other single thing because money is of first importance when it comes to a man's real nature. Money is an exact index to a man's true character. All through Scripture there is an intimate correlation between the development of a man's character and how he handles his money."[3]

The Faithful Use of Money Relates to the Quality of Our Spiritual Life. The way you handle your money has eternal spiritual consequences. In the words of Martin Luther, "There are three conversions: the conversion of the heart, the mind, and the purse." The Bible says,

For unless you are honest in small matters, you won't be in the large ones. If you cheat even a little, you won't be honest with greater responsibilities. And if you are untrustworthy about worldly wealth, who will trust you with the true riches of heaven?

Luke 16:10, 11

Here, Jesus equated a man's ability to handle financial matters with the quality of his spiritual life. He said if a man is faithful in one, he is going to be faithful in the other. Only as we properly relate to our possessions can we properly relate to our God.

The Faithful Use of Money Leads to Contentment. In the previous chapter we left a contented Daniel in the lions' den. He was content for two reasons: 1) Daniel knew that God was in absolute control of the circumstances and that God was capable of delivering him; 2) Daniel had done everything he could by being a good and faithful steward. So his conscience was clean.

They began trying to find a ground of accusation against Daniel in regard to government affairs; but they could find no ground of accusation or evidence of corruption, inasmuch as he was faithful, and no negligence or corruption was to be found in him.

Daniel 6:4, NASB

In Philippians we discover that Paul has learned to be content because: 1) He knew that God would supply all his needs (Philippians 4:19) and 2) He had been a faithful steward. "The things you have learned and received and heard and *seen in me*, practice these things" (Philippians 4:9, NASB).

The Bible offers contentment and in the process, it suggests real solutions to the financial problems of the twentieth century. The rest of this book is about these practical solutions. Each chapter deals with one of the nine specific areas necessary to equip us to become faithful stewards.

CONTRAST

Society says: Do your own thing. You earned your money, now spend it any way you like and you'll be happy.

Scripture says: You can only be content if you have been a faithful steward.

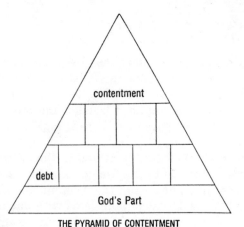

THE PYRAMID OF CONTENTMENT

FIVE
DEBT—
ACT YOUR OWN WAGE

Any government, like any family, can for a year spend a little more than it earns. But you and I know that a continuance of that habit means the poorhouse.
                                        Franklin D. Roosevelt, 1932

. . . free from the dominion of vice; by the practice of industry and frugality, free from debt, which exposes a man to confinement, and slavery to his creditors.
                              Benjamin Franklin, Eighteenth century

Just as the rich rule the poor, so the borrower is servant to the lender.
                                        King Solomon, Tenth century, B.C.

The most immediate financial problem facing Allen and Jean was pressure from their creditors. And creditors they had. Their debts totaled more than $9,000, not including the $37,500 house mortgage. They had two loans from a bank, one from a finance company, bills from three department stores, and $3,500 owed on an assortment of eleven credit cards.

The Hitchcocks' indebtedness started soon after they had married when they applied for their first loan. Jean, who grew up in a wealthy family, said, "Our friends had new cars, and we felt deprived. We had to have a new car too."

Later, when they were transferred to Orlando, they impulsively bought a house in the suburbs, borrowing $3,000 from a bank for the down payment. They increased the bank loan to $3,500 when they began to fall behind on mortgage payments. The debts piled up. Jean said, "The man from the bank told us he was going to take our house and garnishee [take over] Allen's salary."

"Most of our debts were accumulated so slowly through the years," Allen said, "we didn't realize what was happening until it was too late."

CREEPING CREDIT

Like the Hitchcocks, many families in debt get there so slowly that they do not realize it until it becomes an overwhelming problem. Let us examine how creeping credit sneaks up on a family that spends just $3.35 a day ($100 a month) more than it earns. Assume an average interest charge of 12 percent compounded monthly for ten years.

Year	Amount Overspent	Accumulated Interest	Ending Balance
1	$ 1,200	$ 70	$ 1,270
2	1,200	300	2,700
3	1,200	700	4,300
4	1,200	1,300	6,100
5	1,200	2,200	8,200
6	1,200	3,300	10,500
7	1,200	4,600	13,000
8	1,200	6,400	16,000
9	1,200	8,500	19,300
10	1,200	11,000	23,000
Total	$12,000	$11,000	$23,000

At the end of 10 years the family that overspends $3.35 a day owes a total of $23,000! Interest charges alone amount to $230 a month. Beware of creeping credit.

Each year millions of Americans find themselves in the Hitchcocks' predicament. One out of every twenty families that takes out a loan to buy a new car or uses a credit card to purchase school clothes for the children will have trouble making payments. A credit expert says the major reason is "damage to the borrower's ability to pay." People take out loans based on the assumption of a steady flow of income, and the "unexpected happens." People get sick. The wife gets pregnant. An employer closes shop.

For almost a quarter of a million Americans each year the burden of debt is so great that they declare bankruptcy. In a credit-dependent economy like that of the United States, it is not surprising that bankruptcy is a common occurrence.

CREDIT INCREASING

"With so much credit around, you're bound to have casualties," Vern Countryman, a Harvard professor, explains. "It's just like auto accidents. If you're going to have all those cars, you're going to have accidents."

The president of Consumer Credit Counseling Service of Greater New York describes his clients as people who supplement their income with credit. More than ever, the American economy is riding on a growing mountain of debt. The cash-on-the-barrelhead society has become the credit society, and the practice of buying only what can be paid for in cash is as out of style as the crew cut or bobby socks.

Credit was once the exclusive privilege of the well-to-do, but the consumer picture has dramatically changed. That tough, demanding banker who required that your grandfather produce good collateral before he received a loan has been replaced by the friendly financial advisor who can plan your future and help you relax with those easy monthly payments!

Americans have responded by borrowing like never before—first for their home, then for their car and refrigerator, and finally for their pleasure—items such as television sets and vacations—from the most durable to the least durable. The variety of goods and services available on credit is unlimited.

Statistics prepared by the Federal Reserve show that consumer installment debt has multiplied more than thirty-one times since 1945. Personal debts have reached a point where it takes approximately one dollar out of every four that consumers earn (after taxes) to keep up the payments.

Moreover, there are now 85 million holders of Visa and Master Charge cards and new approvals for Visa and Master Charge average 75,000 a day.

BORROWING AS A WAY OF LIFE

Obviously, borrowing has become a way of life for most Americans. Credit cards, charge accounts, and loans are so commonplace now that Americans feel it is their right to borrow and charge as they pursue the Great American Dream. It is a dream characterized by the accumulation of wealth and possessions which are supposed to bring a comfortable, secure style of living. Year after year the American Dream becomes more and more attractive as new and better merchandise is advertised as the evidence of prosperity. And year after year Americans are determined to buy that dream with or without money. Borrowing has moved from a position of disrespect to respectability.

A respected magazine recently carried an article under the heading of "The Wisdom of Debt" in which it was said, "It may come as a shock to those of us raised with old-fashioned attitudes about money, but the adage, 'Neither a borrower nor a lender be,' simply has no place in today's economy. William Flanagan, contributing editor of *Esquire* on financial matters, has suggested a new maxim: 'Get thee in hock.'

"We should take our cue from major corporations, Flanagan suggests. The corporations themselves are constantly in debt—'They'd be insane to operate on a no-debt basis.'

"Nor is the new maxim just for the wealthy. Even

middle-income people who think they're up to their debt limit probably have considerable unused equity they should be putting to work.

"This sort of thinking is hard for many Americans to get used to. 'Sure, it seems like blasphemy,' Flanagan says, 'but the logic of it is inescapable. You only have to examine the facts!' "[4]

Well, let's examine the facts of those "easy monthly payments."

EASY MONTHLY PAYMENTS

It sounds so easy, so attractive: "Introducing: the best friend your checking account ever had." "Relax: now there's an easy solution to those nagging money problems." "Buy now: and pay later with a small monthly payment."

Have these credit card companies and banks finally come up with a quick, painless answer to your financial problems? No, they are merely presenting the positive, and temporary, aspects of instant credit.

THE REAL DEFINITION OF DEBT

These solutions add up to one word which the advertisers neglect to mention: debt.

With ad agencies, the government, and borrowers trying to find more attractive definitions for debt, we'd best examine an objective list of synonyms for debt from the *Roget's College Thesaurus:* answerable for; in embarrassed circumstances; liable; chargeable; in difficulties; unrewarded; deeply involved; minus; owing; in hock; up against it; encumbered; plunged into debt; insolvent.

Did you feel uncomfortable as you read this list? I have yet to see one ad that promises the good life of "buy now and pay later" balanced with one of these words that describe the reality of debt.

Are you beginning to have the feeling that the "gospel

according to Madison Avenue" might not be preaching the whole truth of the abundant life as a member of the debt set?

A 1975 study sponsored by General Mills, Inc. found that although 60 percent of 1,200 families interviewed felt that being debt-free was a "very important personal value," two-thirds of those used credit for daily expenses. The study found that people reconciled this contradiction by changing the definition of debt from "owing money" to the euphemistic "falling behind in payments."

Nowhere in Scripture is debt specifically defined. But in my opinion you are in debt when either of the following circumstances are true:

1) *Money is owed with payments due.* For instance, if you purchased merchandise on a credit card with funds set aside to pay for the entire billing at the end of the month, then you are not in debt. However, if you are unable to pay the entire billing and carry a balance due, then I think you have qualified to be a member of the debt set.

2) *When the amount owed (liability) exceeds the asset value of an item.* For example, if you purchase a new car for $4,000 with $200 cash down and finance the remaining $3,800, then you are in debt because a car depreciates substantially the moment you drive it out of the showroom. Even if you sold the car, the cash proceeds would not be enough to cover the amount owed. This is true with almost any depreciating asset—furniture, clothes, boats, etc.

VIEW OF DEBT IN SCRIPTURE

The Bible speaks point-blank to the subject of debt. "Keep out of debt and owe no man anything, except to love one another" (Romans 13:8, Amplified).

I like this translation because it reads like a road sign—Keep Out of Debt. Is there any wonder why it wasn't too many years ago that it was considered a sin for a Christian to be in debt? The writer of Proverbs explains the reason God speaks so directly to the principle of staying out of debt. "Just as the rich rule the poor, so the borrower is servant to the lender" (22:7).

When you are in debt you have lost a degree of your freedom, and the deeper you are in debt the more freedom you have lost. When payments drag on for months and years, when finance charges and interest rates eat away at your paychecks, when you are unable to give sacrificially to the Lord because you are paying sacrificially for your possessions, and when your paycheck is allotted to bill payments before you even get hold of it, then you are in financial bondage to the lender.

Now situations arise when it may be necessary to borrow. These situations should be prayerfully entered into with wisdom and counsel. We will discuss these situations in the next chapter.

I should warn you: if you are out of debt, those around you will look at you as some kind of radical. But the truth is that getting out and staying out of debt is essential in being faithful stewards and in reaching our goal of contentment.

CONTRAST

Society says: Buy now and pay later with those easy monthly payments.

Scripture says: "Keep out of debt" (Romans 13:8).

SIX
GETTING OUT OF DEBT—
"D" DAY

The modern American is a person who drives a
bank-financed car over a bond-financed highway on
credit-card gas to open a charge account at a department
store so he can fill his savings-and-loan financed home
with installment-purchased furniture.

"I hope I never pick up another one," Allen said.

"I just didn't know," Jean recalled. "I had no
experience."

What were they talking about? Poisonous reptiles?
Radioactive material? Hard drugs?

No. Credit cards. The Hitchcocks had run up $3,500 on
eleven credit cards and were paying 18 percent in interest
for that "privilege."

This is a common predicament in America today. The
easy availability of credit has spawned a phenomenal
growth in the number of cards held by customers.
Americans hold 590 million cards and the average
American consumer packs away more than five cards in
his wallet.

Business Today magazine told of the most avid credit
card collector in the country. Earlier this year, Walter
Cavanaugh, a pharmacist with an annual income of about

$27,000, said he owned approximately 800 credit cards. He collects them for fun and routinely stores all but a few in a safe-deposit box. If Cavanaugh actually used his 800-plus cards, however, he would have an estimated line of credit approaching $9.3 million in a single month.[5]

At the end of the initial conference with the Hitchcocks, Allen asked for my scissors. He wanted to perform some "plastic surgery." As a symbol of their vow to get out of debt, he cut their credit cards to ribbons. If they follow through in their commitment, they will be in the minority. Less than 50 percent of those who take the initial step actually follow through on their commitment and reach the goal of becoming debt-free.

The reason is that it is painful and often tedious work to get out of debt. Simply to stop overspending is not enough. A three-step reduction is required in your spending habits:

1) Stop spending more than you make.
2) Pay the interest on the debt.
3) Repay the debt.

Do you see why there is nothing easy about those "easy monthly payments"? Getting out of debt is often an awesome task, so awesome that I believe most debtors require a stronger motivation than just the desire to be debt-free. The best motivator is a desire to conform to Scripture:

Evil men borrow and "cannot pay it back"! But the good man returns what he owes with some extra besides.
Psalm 37:21

Don't withhold repayment of your debts. Don't say "some other time," if you can pay now.
Proverbs 3:27, 28

The Bible clearly calls us to start getting out of debt as quickly as we can. It is never easy, but it is the Lord's desire for us to be free from the servitude of debt, and all things are possible with God.

STEPS FOR GETTING OUT OF DEBT

The path for getting out of debt will be an individual one because of your own particular circumstances. The following eight steps are a guide for your journey.

The steps are simple. What is hard is the dogged persistence required to follow through, all the way, until you reach your destination—freedom from indebtedness.

Establish a Written Budget. A written budget is the first and most important step in getting out of debt because it is a plan for spending money. Thus you can use a budget to schedule your debt-reduction and to monitor progress.

A budget can also help you analyze your spending patterns to see where you can cut back, and it is an effective bridle on impulse spending.

Make a List of All Your Assets. List every asset you own: your home, car, furniture, cash, etc. See the Asset List below for a guideline.

ASSET LIST—WHAT IS OWNED

1. CASH AND ASSETS EASILY
   CONVERTIBLE TO CASH
   (a) Cash   _____
   (b) Stocks (Market Value)   _____
   (c) Bonds   _____
   (d) Cash value of life insurance
       (call agent)   _____
   (e) Coins   _____
2. REAL ESTATE
   (a) Home (market value)   _____
   (b) Other real estate   _____
3. RECEIVABLES
   (a) Mortgage receivables   _____
   (b) Notes receivables   _____
4. OTHER INVESTMENTS   _____
5. AUTOMOBILES (call dealer for today's
   value)   _____

6   PERSONAL PROPERTY*
    (a) Furniture   _____
    (b) Boats   _____
    (c) Cameras   _____
    (d) Hobbies   _____
    (e) Other   _____
7. ACCRUED RETIREMENT BENEFITS   _____

    TOTAL ASSETS   _____

*Personal property is the most difficult of assets to evaluate. Appraise as
conservatively as possible because the depreciated value of second-hand personal
property is ordinarily quite low.

Evaluate the completed list to determine whether you
should sell any assets. As we began to consider items the
Hitchcocks might sell, the most obvious one was their new
second car.

"I can't do without my car, Allen," Jean protested.

Allen looked hurt and guilty. He didn't want to deprive
his wife of anything she wanted, but they both realized
that some drastic action was necessary.

By deciding to sell the car *and* Allen's gun collection,
the Hitchcocks cut their indebtedness $3,000 and began to
use the amount of the car payment for some of their other
debts. As George Fooshee has said, "Your attitude toward
things will determine your success in working your way
out of debt. Don't think about how much you will lose of
what you paid for the item you are selling. Think about
how much you will gain which can be applied to your debt
reduction immediately."[6]

Make a List of All Your Debts.   It came as a surprise to
me that most people don't have a clear picture of what
they owe. List all of your debts (including those to
relatives), with the monthly payment required and the
annual rate of interest.

DEBT LIST—WHAT IS OWED

	Monthly payment	Interest rate	Balance due
1. HOME MORTGAGE			
2. CREDIT CARD COMPANIES			
3. BANK			
4. INSTALLMENT LOANS			
5. LOAN COMPANIES			
6. INSURANCE COMPANIES			
7. CREDIT UNION			
8. LOANS FROM RELATIVES			
9. OTHER PERSONAL LOANS			
10. BUSINESS LOANS			
11. MEDICAL LOANS			
12. OTHERS			
TOTAL DEBTS			

As you will discover from analyzing the interest rates on your debt list, credit costs vary greatly: from as little as 9 percent a year for a loan from a credit union, to 12 percent for a bank loan, to 18 percent for credit cards, to 20 percent and up for installment purchases, to 25–36 percent from a finance or small-loan company.

The listing of your debts will assist you in establishing a priority for reducing your indebtedness—try to retire the highest interest rate debts first.

Establish a Debt Repayment Schedule.   These steps for getting out of debt may seem tedious, but they are absolutely necessary. Nobody ever gets out of debt by accident.

We all need a systematic written payment schedule to reach the goal of "D-Day"—"debtless day."

A typical repayment schedule looks something like this:

REPAYMENT SCHEDULE

Creditor_____

	Monthly payment	Months remaining	Balance due
January	_____	_____	_____
February	_____	_____	_____
March	_____	_____	_____

After you have made your monthly payments, write down the amount paid and compute the balance due. Recording your payments will give you a sense of accomplishment and watching the balance diminish will give you the incentive that will help you persist in your plan.

If you are deeply in debt or have been past due on your payments to creditors, it is a good idea to take or send them a copy of your repayment schedule. It is the rare creditor who will not go along with a person making a serious effort to systematically pay his debt. They will appreciate the fact that you have made out a schedule and have been concerned enough to share it with them.

As you pay off a creditor, begin to apply that payment to another debt to more quickly reduce your total indebtedness.

Apply Additional Income.　Another way to expedite your freedom from debt is to agree in advance to apply any additional income to the repayment of debt. This includes such income as overtime pay, income tax refunds, garage sale earnings, odd jobs, payments, or any other income.

Jean Hitchcock proved to be a very industrious and creative person. She started a "mini-nursery" in her home, baby-sitting four children from her neighborhood during the day while the parents worked. The two older Hitchcock children were also encouraged to babysit in the evenings, and they contributed half of their earnings to the family's debt reduction.

In fact, Jean and the two children were able to

contribute $135 a week (more than $500 a month) to the repayment of debt!

This is only one of hundreds of imaginative ways to earn additional income to get out of debt more quickly. The key when earning extra money is to ensure that it will be applied to the reduction of debt and not to a higher level of spending.

Accumulate No New Debts.   A foolproof way to do this is to only pay for things with cash. Don't use credit cards. Somehow they give people the feeling that they're not spending real money—it's just "funny money." Like the shopper who said to a friend, "I like credit cards; they go so much farther than cash!" It has been proved that the family that uses credit cards will spend more money. Beware of plastic money!

Be Content With What You Have.

The advertising industry has developed powerful and sophisticated tools aimed at creating discontentment in our lives. For example, advertising on television has a big impact on people because the average American watches television twenty hours a week. By the time the typical teen-ager graduates from high school, he has spent 10,800 hours in class and 15,000 hours in front of the tube. The average one-half hour of television viewing has thirteen commercials, which means that the average American watches between fifty and a hundred commercials a day. Advertising is designed for one purpose—to encourage us to buy something by creating in us a lack of contentment with what we already have.

A large manufacturing firm decided to open a new assembly plant in an underdeveloped Latin American country because labor was cheap and plentiful. The plant was successfully opened and the operation was progressing smoothly—until the first paycheck. The next day, none of the villagers reported for work.

Management waited . . . one, two, three days. Still no villagers came to work. The plant manager went to see

the village chief to find out the problem. "Why should we
continue to work?" the chief asked in response to the
manager's inquiry. "We are satisfied. We have already
earned all the money we need to live on."

The plant stood idle for almost a month. Then someone
came up with the idea of distributing Sears catalogs to all
the villagers. Reading the catalogs created new needs in
the lives of the villagers. Since that time there has not
been an unemployment problem.

Here are four axioms: 1) The more shopping we do, the
more we spend; 2) The more we watch television, the more
we spend; 3) The more time we spend looking through
catalogs, the more we spend; 4) The more we read
magazines and newspaper advertisements, the more we
spend.

It is much easier to remain content with what you
have if you purposely avoid the temptations caused by
advertising.

Do Not Give Up!   Recognize from the beginning there will
be a hundred logical reasons why you should quit or delay
your efforts to get out of debt.

Don't! Don't! Don't!

Don't stop until you have reached the marvelous goal
of freedom from debt. Remember, getting out of debt is
just plain hard work, but the blessings of contentment are
worth the struggle.

WHEN CAN WE OWE MONEY?

Scripture does not tell us whether we can legitimately
borrow money for any specific assets or purposes, so this
section is strictly my own opinion. Please critically
examine this issue, then prayerfully reach your own
conclusion.

I believe money should only be borrowed for four
items*:

---

*Note: the automobile is not included in the list of items for which money can
be borrowed. However, there are circumstances in which a person may borrow for
an automobile. These are discussed in the chapter, Questions and Answers.

1) Home
2) Business
3) Education
4) Certain types of investments

I also believe that before you borrow for any of these items three criteria should be met:

1) Borrowing should be limited to appreciating assets or assets that produce an income.

2) The value of the asset should equal or exceed the amount borrowed to acquire the item.

3) The amount borrowed should be within your ability to repay without placing a strain on your budget.

Let me illustrate how these criteria work in the purchase of a house. The family house has historically been an appreciating asset. It meets our first criterion. Second, if a house is purchased with a reasonable down payment, then its value will be greater than the mortgage. To meet the third criterion, the house purchased should not be so expensive that the monthly payments are too difficult to meet. If all three criteria are met, then in my opinion borrowing can be justified.

But be careful. Even if all the criteria are satisfied, the borrower still is a "servant" who is obligated to the lender. Meeting the criteria only improves your chances of repaying the debt. It is not a guarantee.

For this reason, several years ago Bev and I decided to begin to repay all the money we had borrowed—even the mortgage on our home. Progress has been slow, but it has been extremely satisfying. God as been steadily providing the additional income necessary to repay most of the money we had borrowed.

You may decide on a similar goal. If you do, it is a good strategy to first eliminate those debts that do not qualify under these criteria. Then begin to systematically make payments against the remaining money borrowed.

It is a long, hard process. So do not become discouraged. For most people, it has to be a long-term goal (ten to fifteen years) because the debts and house mortgage are usually large. I encourage you to prayerfully consider such a goal.

COSIGNING

Cosigning relates to borrowing. When you cosign, you pledge your assets against the debt of another. Scripture refers to this as "surety" or "striking hands." Any time you cosign, you must be prepared for total loss of the amount for which you have obligated yourself.

Scripture's perspective of cosigning is best summed up in Proverbs 17:18, "It is poor judgment to countersign another's note, to become responsible for his debts."

The Hebrew words for "poor judgment" are translated "destitute of mind." We can confidently say that the biblical norm is to avoid cosigning.

The dangers of cosigning are even more graphically illustrated in Proverbs 22:26, 27: "Unless you have the extra cash on hand, don't countersign a note. Why risk everything you own? They'll even take your bed!"

This passage presents an almost comical picture of the creditor pulling the cosigner's bed out from underneath him. I said *almost* comical, because as I was reading this verse to a friend he responded, "I know what you mean! As I came home one evening from work, my neighbor was having every stick of furniture, including his bed, taken from him. He had cosigned on a note that had gone sour. At the time that he cosigned he just had not understood the liability he was assuming and, in fact, he had forgotten all about it."

When you cosign a note, your liability is just as great as if you had borrowed the money yourself. The lender has refused to make the loan to the person for whom you are cosigning because his credit is not good enough. But your credit and your collateral are sufficient security on the loan.

You are involving yourself in a loan that is too great a risk for the professional lender. You are counting on your friend or relative to pay back the loan, but unfortunately they frequently will not. Lenders tell us that approximately 50 percent of all cosigners end up paying.

When the friend or relative defaults, then the cosigner has the "privilege" of paying the debt—something for which cosigners seldom plan. I believe that Scripture counsels us against cosigning because it is simply another way to become entangled by debt.

CONTRAST

Society says: A family can comfortably carry 15 to 20 percent of its take-home pay in debt. Buy now and pay later with those easy monthly payments. After all, it's not as if you can't afford it. You are simply using the item while paying for it.

Scripture says: Get out of debt and stay out of debt.

COMMITMENT

As a family, formalize your desire to get out of debt. Then follow the eight guidelines of becoming debt-free. A helpful method of sticking to your plan is to seek the counsel of some friend or friends who can hold you accountable.

The value of seeking advice is the subject of the next chapter.

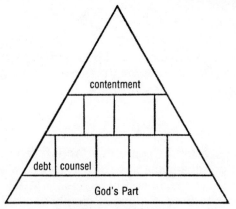

THE PYRAMID OF CONTENTMENT

SEVEN
COUNSEL—
A TRIPLE-BRAIDED CORD

Two can accomplish more than twice as much as one.
Ecclesiastes 4:9

*And one standing alone can be attacked and defeated, but
two can stand back-to-back and conquer; three is even
better, for a triple-braided cord is not easily broken.*
Ecclesiastes 4:12

The scene was like something you might have read about
in the stories of the Arabian nights. King Xerxes—that
most extravagant Persian emperor—held a grandiose
celebration to display his tremendous wealth and power.
The climax to this six-month revelry was an exclusive
week-long party for his palace staff.

The setting was lavish beyond belief. "The decorations
were tied to silver rings imbedded in marble pillars. Gold
and silver benches stood on pavements of black, red,
white, and yellow marble. Drinks were served in golden
goblets of many designs, and there was an abundance of
royal wine" (Esther 1:6, 7).

As the revelry intensified, a half-drunk King Xerxes
ordered his queen to appear so that his guests could gaze
upon her great beauty, but she refused.

Note his reaction. "The king was furious, but first

consulted his lawyers, for he did nothing without their advice. They were men of wisdom who knew the temper of the times as well as Persian law and justice, and the king trusted their judgment" (Esther 1:12, 13).

The English expression for the Hebrew word translated "furious" is "red in the throat." His reaction is extraordinary when we consider a half-drunk monarch flushing with anger—"He first consulted his lawyers, for he did nothing without their advice." Xerxes' deeply ingrained habit of seeking advice prevailed even in his drunken rage.

This is a sharp contradiction to our culture's practice. The ideal American is to be a rugged individualist. A man's man. A bigger than life, John Wayne-type who can make all decisions alone and unafraid, and who can cope with any financial pressure in stoic silence. Our culture asserts: Be a man, stand on your own two feet.

Almost 500 years before Xerxes' reign, another king, Solomon, dominated the world scene. Known as "the first great commercial king of Israel," he was a skilled diplomat, and director of extensive building, shipping, and mining ventures. However, Solomon is most often remembered as the wisest king who ever lived. In fact, he made wisdom a subject of study.

In Proverbs he wrote, "Wisdom is better than jewels, and all that you desire cannot compare with her. Happy is the man who finds wisdom, and the man who gets understanding, for the gain of it is better than gain from silver and its profit better than gain from gold."

Solomon's practical recommendations on embracing wisdom are also found in Proverbs: "Get all the advice you can and be wise" (19:20). "A fool thinks he needs no advice, but a wise man listens to others" (12:15). "Listen to counsel. Oh, don't refuse it, and become wise" (8:33).

FROM WHOM DO WE SEEK COUNSEL?

Scripture encourages us to seek counsel from three sources. First, from the Lord himself. In fact, one of the names he calls himself is Wonderful Counselor. Second, seek counsel from the Bible. "Your laws are both my light and my counselors" (Psalm 119:24). Lastly, we are urged to seek the counsel of godly people. "The godly man is a good counselor because he is just and fair and knows right from wrong" (Psalm 37:30, 31).

THE BODY

The Apostle Paul recognized the benefit of godly counsel. After he was converted on the Damascus Road, he never was alone in his public ministry. He knew and appreciated the value of a couple of extra sets of eyes looking down that straight and narrow road. Timothy, Barnabas, Luke, or someone else was always with him.

In fact, in the New Testament *saint* is never used in the singular. It is always in the plural. Someone has described the Christian life as not one of independence from each other, but of dependence upon each other. Nowhere is this more clearly illustrated than in Paul's discussion concerning the Body of Christ in the 12th chapter of 1 Corinthians.

Each of us is pictured as a different member of this body. And our ability to function normally is dependent upon the members working together. God has given each individual certain abilities and gifts, but God has not given any one person all the ability that he needs to operate alone at his optimum level. As someone has said, "Every meeting of persons is an exchange of talents and gifts."

Further, we are specifically encouraged to seek the advice of friends, older and more experienced people, and parents. And if you are married, your spouse is to be your primary source of human counsel. A husband and wife are one.

You need to consult and train your spouse in all family financial matters. I have done this, and it has been a pleasant surprise for me to observe how astute Bev's analysis has been concerning finances. Even though her formal education has not been related to business, she has developed excellent business sense, and her decisions are often better than mine.

COUNSEL TO BE AVOIDED

Scripture speaks directly to the issue of avoiding those counselors who are not godly. "How blessed is the man who does not walk in the counsel of the wicked" (Psalm 1:1, NASB).

In my opinion, we can seek specific technical assistance, such as legal and accounting advice, from those who do not know God. But armed with the technical data, counsel for making the final decision should be limited to those who know the Lord.

BIG DECISIONS

Some decisions, because of their importance and permanence, deserve more attention than others. Decisions concerning marriage and career, for example, affect us for a longer period of time than most other choices we make in life.

When getting advice on such important issues, we should try to obtain advice from a variety of counselors. "Plans go wrong with too few counselors; many counselors bring success" (Proverbs 15:22).

Frankly, I had not fully appreciated the benefits of seeking the counsel of many until writing this book. Twelve people critiqued the manuscript and each made a significant contribution. I was overwhelmed how a diversity of opinion improved its content and quality.

A practical way of applying the principle of many counselors is to become involved in a small group.

OUR SMALL GROUP

Bev and I have met with three other couples on a regular basis for several years, and we have become mutual counselors. We don't make a major decision without seeking the advice of those friends. And believe me, our small group has been through some traumatic times together. Five babies, two job changes, two new businesses, home and car purchases, marital conflicts, and financial pressures have marked the last four years.

We have rejoiced together during each others'

successes, and comforted and wept with each other during the hard times. The advice of these friends has not only benefited our checkbook, but has significantly contributed to our emotional and spiritual health.

We are convinced that there is great value in maintaining an ever-deepening relationship with at least one person who can be a counselor. A person who knows you well can be your most effective counselor.

It has been a struggle to keep the relationships in our group growing, but the encouragement and accountability inherent in an intimate relationship are worth the effort. It is a practical way to motivate each other to adhere to God's principles of how to handle money.

WHAT'S A BODY TO DO?

Another practical method of getting counsel is to be exposed to an individual who has the special ability to give good counsel. "To one person the Spirit gives the ability to give wise advice" (1 Corinthians 12:8).

I believe each church or body should try to identify those in their midst who have this talent, and then encourage them to exercise their ability for the benefit of the other members.

Jim Seneff has this ability. He has served many in our church, including myself, as an outstanding counselor. I cannot adequately express how grateful I am for his guidance.

As a competent businessman, Jim is aware of financial planning, good management techniques, and trends in the economy. His assistance in each area has been considerable. But even more valuable has been his skillful questioning of my life goals which has helped me rethink many areas of life.

Thus, I can heartly agree with the words of Solomon, "One standing alone can be attacked and defeated, but two can stand back-to-back and conquer; three is even better, for a triple-braided cord is not easily broken" (Ecclesiastes 4:12).

CONTRAST

Society says: Be a man, stand on your own two feet. You don't need anyone to tell you what to do.

Scripture says: "The wise man is glad to be instructed, but a self-sufficient fool falls flat on his face" (Proverbs 10:8).

COMMITMENT

In my experience, the vast majority of those persons in financial difficulties have not followed the scriptural admonishment of seeking wise counsel. They have been molded by our culture's view that admitting a need and seeking advice is only for those who are not strong enough to be self-sufficient.

More often than not, a person's pride is the biggest deterrent to seeking advice. This is especially true if we are facing a personal financial crisis. It is embarrassing to expose our problems to someone else.

Another reason for reluctance to seek counsel is the fear that an objective evaluation of our finances may surface issues we would rather avoid: a lack of disciplined spending, an unrealistic budget, a lack of communication in the family, or the suggestion to give up something dear to us.

I cannot over-emphasize the importance of counsel, and I encourage you to evaluate your situation. If you do not have a counselor, try to cultivate a friendship with at least one godly person who can advise you.

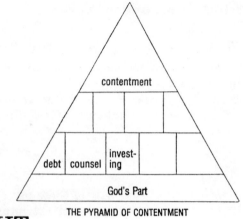

THE PYRAMID OF CONTENTMENT

EIGHT
INVESTING—
STEADY PLODDING

The wise man saves for the future, but the foolish man spends whatever he gets.

Proverbs 21:20

Faithful stewardship demands a balance between trusting God and taking steps to plan for future needs.

"The average American family is three weeks away from bankruptcy," a recent article declared. "The average family has little or no money saved, a large amount of fixed monthly living expenses and credit obligations, and total dependence upon next month's income to remain solvent."

Similarly, a Social Security Administration study revealed that half of non-married men ages fifty-eight to sixty-three had financial assets of less than $470. This startling fact was confirmed during a seminar in Indiana. We stayed with a family that operates a number of nursing homes. Sixty-five percent of their patients are fully subsidized by the government. To qualify for government assistance, the patient cannot have a net worth of more than $700.

These statistics indicate that many people have not

followed God's principles for saving. In fact, the United States has the lowest rate of saving among the wealthy countries of the world.

Indeed, saving and investing are sometimes considered taboo subjects—something that spiritual people should avoid discussing. Many Christians seem to have the idea that to save means not to trust in God for his provision. This is not correct.

This chapter deals with the practical application of Scripture to savings, investing, lending, inheritance, and wills.

SAVING—THE JOSEPH PRINCIPLE

A skillful steward divides his income among sharing, spending, and saving. "The wise man saves for the future but the foolish man spends whatever he gets" (Proverbs 21:20).

Because of their instinct for saving, the ants in Proverbs 30:24 are commended for their wisdom: "There are . . . things that are small but usually wise: Ants aren't strong, but store up food for the winter." They put aside and save from the summer's plenty to meet a future need.

Another example is Joseph, the faithful steward, who saved from the seven years of plenty to insure that there would be food enough to eat during the seven years of famine.

I call saving the "Joseph Principle." Saving means to forego an expenditure today so that you will have something to spend in the future. Perhaps this is why most people never save; it requires a denial of something that you want today, and our culture is not a culture of denial. Because it is a culture of instant gratification, most people spend their entire income.

Saving is important in faithful financial planning for three reasons. First, saving provides a cushion to meet unexpected events—loss of employment, major repair bills, and sudden illness. Second, savings should be accumulated to enable you to purchase your car, furniture, etc., without

having to use credit. And third, accumulated savings
provide a pool of resources for investing.

HOW TO SAVE

The essential rule for saving is to make yourself your
number one creditor after the Lord. Habitually save a
portion of your income, putting it into a savings account
or savings program. The percentage of your income that
you save does not matter. What is important is that you
establish a pattern of regular savings.

To develop this habit you can use several different
methods. For example, before we spend anything Bev and
I set aside a certain percent of our income each month in
a savings account. It might be easier for you to use one of
the compulsory savings plans that are available through
most banks, or an employee payroll plan. Here is a maxim
for saving: If the money budgeted for saving is deducted
directly from your paycheck, you will save more.

As you begin to save, you will discover what bankers
have known for a long time—the benefits of interest,
money working for you, not against you.

Let us examine how money works for the family that
saves. Assume saving $100 a month and receiving 8
percent interest, compounded monthly for twenty-five
years.

MONEY WORKING FOR YOU AT 8 PERCENT INTEREST

Year	Amount Saved	Interest Earned	Ending Balance
1	$ 1,200	$ 45	$ 1,245
2	1,200	200	2,600
3	1,200	450	4,050
4	1,200	850	5,650
5	1,200	1,350	7,350
6	1,200	2,000	9,200
7	1,200	2,800	11,200

8	1,200	3,800	13,400
9	1,200	5,000	15,750
10	1,200	6,300	18,300
10 year Subtotal	12,000	6,300	18,300
15	1,200	16,600	34,600
20	1,200	34,900	58,900
25	1,200	65,100	95,100
Total	$30,000	$65,100	$95,100

At the end of twenty-five years the family will be earning $635 each month in interest alone! What an incentive to begin saving.

For an even greater incentive to save, compare the results of spending $100 more than you earn each month for 10 years with spending $100 less than you earn each month. Should you spend $100 more each month you will *owe* $23,000; spend $100 less and you will *own* $18,300—a staggering difference of $41,300 at the end of ten years!

The difference between overspending $100 and saving $100 a month is $6.50 a day.

This illustrates the importance of a disciplined commitment to save. The difference between sinking in debt and walking on the firm ground of savings is a matter of a few cents each day.

The biggest enemy of saving is *procrastination*. For instance, if you plan to save $100 a month for 25 years at 8 percent, you will accumulate more than $95,000. However, look what happens if you decide to delay such a program by one year. Although you will have an extra $100 a month to spend for one year, it will cost you $8,500 in accumulated savings on the other end. Do not wait—begin to save now!

INVESTING

Investments differ from saving in that they are not always quickly convertible to cash, and they represent a conscious effort to provide for specific future events or as a hedge to beat inflation. For example, college for children and funding for retirement represent future expenditures that may be planned and financed from current income.

HOW SHOULD WE INVEST?

There is no investment without risk, and Scripture does not recommend any specific investments. I prefer to spread the risk by diversifying according to these priorities: 1) life insurance, 2) vocation, 3) house, and 4) other investments.

George Fooshee in his excellent book, *You Can Be Financially Free*, says, "The first priority is life insurance because that's the only way for most of us to provide for our families in the event of our own death. Whether you buy term insurance or whole-life insurance should depend upon your own analysis of the costs and the benefits of each kind. An excellent article on the subject is 'Term Insurance vs. Whole Life' (*Forbes*, March 15, 1975). What is right for one person may be wrong for another.

"Your vocation should rank next as an investment. Your own education is an investment that should pay excellent returns during your working years. A principle in Scripture is to invest in your business, which will be productive, then build your house: 'Develop your business first before building your house' (Proverbs 24:27). Many people today reverse this order. The large house, purchased early in life, tends to involve so much of their money that investing in their vocation is out of the question.

"The home is the third priority. During the last few decades, the home has been one of the steadiest profitable investments for the average family.

"Other investments (fourth priority) are almost as varied as the imagination. Real estate, oil, commodities, stocks, bonds, antiques, coins, and virtually anything people collect can be considered investments. Some of these, such as stocks, bonds, and real estate, pay a return on an annual basis. Others are held with the expectation that they will increase in value as time goes by.

"Your investments beyond life insurance, vocation, and house should be matched with your own interests and personality. If you were raised on a farm and have knowledge of agricultural products and enjoy keeping abreast of the farm situation, then you might pursue a lifelong interest in agricultural investments. These could include everything from commodity purchases to owning and acquiring farmland. If common stocks are your interest, you might specialize in a study of those companies that are primarily agriculturally oriented.

"All these investments that have been discussed are the kind that lend themselves to systematic investing. The regular monthly payment on the home for a twenty-year mortgage results in having a home completely paid for. Yearly whole-life insurance premiums not only provide insurance in case of death, but also add up to retirement values. Steady hard work in your own business often results in a substantial salable asset. The key to most investments is to set aside regular amounts for systematic investing. 'Steady plodding brings prosperity; hasty speculation brings poverty' (Proverbs 21:5)."[7]

THE DANGER OF SAVING AND INVESTING

As you are successful in accumulating your "nest egg," it is easy to transfer your trust and affection from the invisible living Lord to your tangible assets. Money will certainly compete for your trust and attention. It has so much power that it is easy to be fooled into thinking that it is money which provides our needs and is our security. Money can become our first love. Paul warned Timothy of this temptation in 1 Timothy 6:10, 11.

For the love of money is the first step toward all kinds of sin. Some people have even turned away from God because of their love for it .... Run from all these evil things.

I would like to suggest a radical antidote for the potential disease of loving money: determine a maximum

amount of savings and investments that you will
accumulate.

The amount will vary from individual to individual. If
you are single without any dependents, the amount may
be modest. If you have a family with educational needs, it
may be more substantial. If you are the owner of a sizable
business that requires large amounts of capital, the
amount may be in the millions.

Each person should decide before God what amount
will be his maximum. After you have reached your
maximum goal, begin to *share* the portion of your income
that used to be allocated to savings and investments.

AVOID RISKY INVESTMENTS

The desire to secure large, quick, and effortless returns is
the primary reason for losing money through speculative
investments.

*There is another serious problem I [Solomon] have seen
everywhere—savings are put into risky investments that
turn sour, and soon there is nothing left to pass on to one's
son. The man who speculates is soon back to where he
began—with nothing. This, as I said, is a very serious
problem, for all his hard work has been for nothing; he has
been working for the wind. It is all swept away.*
Ecclesiastes 5:13–15

Scripture clearly warns of avoiding risky investments;
yet each year thousands of people lose money in highly
speculative and sometimes fraudulent investments. How
many times have you heard of "little old ladies" losing
their life's savings on a get-rich-quick scheme? It is not
uncommon.

To help you identify a potentially risky investment, I
have listed eight benefits that often appear in such
schemes.

1. The prospect of a large profit is "practically
guaranteed."

2. The decision to invest must be made quickly. There will be no opportunity to thoroughly investigate the investment or the promoter who is selling the investment.

3. The promoter will have an "excellent track record," and he is doing you a "favor" by allowing you to invest with him.

4. The investment often will offer attractive tax deductions as an incentive.

5. You will know little or nothing about the particular investment.

6. Very little will be said about the risks of losing money.

7. The investment will require no effort on your part.

8. You are going to make a "handsome profit" quickly.

If any potential investment has one or more of these "benefits," it should trigger a red warning light in your mind and alert you to carefully and thoroughly investigate the investment before risking your money.

Before you participate in any investment, seek the wise counsel of those experienced in that particular investment media.

Be patient! I have never known anyone who made money in a hurry. Diligence, study, and counsel are prerequisites for improving your chances for successful investments and for avoiding risky ones.

LENDING

The issue of lending money is divided into two categories: lending as an investment to earn interest, and lending to an individual who is in need.

Lending Money as an Investment to Earn Interest. When you deposit money in a savings account, you are lending the bank money and receiving interest in return. The same is true should you purchase a corporate bond or a U.S. government security or if you loan money to a friend who is starting a new business. You are loaning money to earn interest.

I believe Scripture says this is legitimate and proper. It is clear that it was normal to charge interest on loans:

If you lend money to a needy fellow-Hebrew, you are not to handle the transaction in an ordinary way, with interest.
Exodus 22:25

Then why didn't you deposit the money in the bank so I could at least get interest on it?
Luke 19:23

Lending to Individuals in Need.   God's economy demands that we approach lending to individuals in need in a manner that is contrary to the practice of our culture. In the Old Testament we read that loans to needy fellow-Jews were to be interest-free.

And in the New Testament, not only was the loan to be interest-free, but the lender was not to expect repayment. "And if you lend money only to those who can repay you, what good is that? . . . don't be concerned about the fact that they won't repay" (Luke 6:34, 35).

I want to stress that the interest-free loans that do not require repayment are to be for someone's *needs*—his food, clothing, or shelter. In my opinion, a loan for a person's *wants* can be interest-bearing with repayment expected.

From the lender's standpoint there is no difference between giving to someone in need and lending to his need. In both cases he earns no interest and does not expect repayment. But the recipient's position has changed. A gift requires no repayment, but a loan requires repayment. "Evil men borrow and 'cannot pay it back!' But the good man returns what he owes with some extra besides" (Psalm 37:21).

When someone comes seeking money, how do you know whether to consider giving it or lending it? Matthew 5:42 tells us, "Give to him who asks of you and do not turn away from him who wants to borrow from you." You let the person seeking funds tell you whether he wants a loan or a gift.

Let me give you an example of lending to cement this

issue for you. Two years ago a friend, Kyle Jackson, came to me asking for a loan for a personal need. His request qualified as a need, a basic necessity of life. I told my wife about the request, we prayed about it, and loaned him the money. As far as I was concerned, the money was Kyle's and I never expected repayment. We could continue our relationship without any feelings of guilt or strain if for some reason Kyle was unable to pay back the loan. After six months Kyle asked me out for lunch (which was the "extra besides") and repaid the loan.

Some time later Kyle came and asked for a gift because of a ministry in which he was involved. After I prayed with my wife, we gave him the money. My position had not changed. I still did not expect repayment, but his position had changed.

He is under no obligation before God to repay the gift.

INHERITANCE

Should you leave an inheritance for your children? Yes. "When a good man dies, he leaves an inheritance" (Proverbs 13:22).

You should provide an inheritance for your spouse and children. However, it probably is not wise to leave your children with great wealth if they have not been thoroughly schooled in the biblical perspective of money and how to properly manage it. "The almighty dollar bequeathed to a child is an almighty curse," Andrew Carnegie once said. "No man has the right to handicap his son with such a burden as great wealth. He must face this question squarely: Will the fortune be safe with my boy and will my boy be safe with my fortune?"

"An inheritance gained hurriedly in the beginning will not be blessed in the end" (Proverbs 20:21). The youth who has been trained to be a skillful steward of possessions is a rarity today.

In my opinion you should make provision for distributing an inheritance spread over several years or until the heir is mature enough to handle the responsibility of money. A good idea is to periodically test your children by giving them a small amount of money to see how wisely they use it. If they prove faithful with that small amount, they will be faithful with larger amounts.

WILLS

Seven out of ten of the 1,900,000 Americans who died during 1976 did not have a will.

Think of what this means. To die intestate, without a will, is expensive and time-consuming and can be heartbreaking for your loved ones. It can literally destroy an estate left to provide for the family.

Scripture teaches that we brought nothing into the world and we will take nothing with us when we die. But we *can* leave it behind precisely as we wish—we can specify to whom and how much. If you die without a will, these decisions are left up to the court. Under some circumstances the court can appoint a guardian (who may not know the Lord) to raise your children if you have not made this provision in your will.

At a recent seminar attended by my attorney and his wife, I noticed that his wife was nudging him during the discussion of the necessity of a will. Later I learned that although he had drafted hundreds of wills, including mine, he had not taken the time to draft his own.

Whether you are married, single, rich or poor, you should have a will. Not only does it clear up any legal uncertainties, it also helps you map out your finances while you are alive so that you can protect the best interests of those whom you want to inherit your property.

About thirty-six out of one hundred die before retirement age. So do not put off preparation of your will just because you may be young. Do it now!

CONTRAST

Society says: Spend all you make. However, if you should save, put your trust in your accumulated assets.

Scripture says: "The wise man saves for the future, but the foolish man spends whatever he gets" (Proverbs 21:20).

COMMITMENT

1) Establish a pattern of saving, starting as soon as you receive your next paycheck.
2) Make an appointment with an attorney this week to have your will drawn.

A GUARANTEED INVESTMENT

I stumbled on a guaranteed investment opportunity about six years ago, when I met Jim Seneff and started attending a weekly breakfast with eight young men. I was impressed because they were astute and energetic young businessmen. But more than that, I was impressed by the quality of their lives. I did not know what asset they owned, but whatever it was I wanted it in my portfolio.

At that time I owned a successful restaurant, had married the girl of my dreams, and lived in a nice home. I had everything I thought would give me happiness and a sense of real accomplishment, but somehow I had neither and sensed that something was missing.

I was shocked to learn these men openly called themselves Christians. Frankly, it was just about the most negative thing they could have identified as the source of their most prized possession. I grew up going to church regularly, but somehow missed hearing about the asset of which they spoke—a personal, intimate relationship with Jesus Christ, the Son of the Living God.

A friend of theirs took the time to show me how I could acquire this asset and frankly, the transaction appeared totally inequitable.

I had learned that any time you had two people who were convinced that they were getting more than they were giving up you had a transaction. But now I was being offered a relationship with God and everything I really ever wanted and it was free!

For by grace you have been saved through faith; and that not of yourselves, it is the gift of God; not as a result of works, that no one should boast.
Ephesians 2:8, 9, NASB

This was difficult for me to believe because I had been around the block a few times and had learned that in business there is no such thing as a "free lunch." There always is a price to be paid.

Then my friend described two traits of God: First, God loved me.

God loved the world so much that he gave his only Son so that anyone who believes in him shall not perish but have eternal life.

John 3:16

I could not believe it—God said he actually loved me! The second trait of God's character is that he is holy—which means he is perfect. And a perfect God could not have a personal relationship with anyone who is not also perfect.

My friend then turned his attention to my character by asking if I had ever done anything that would disqualify me for a relationship with a perfect God. "Oh, many times," I admitted. He told me that God loved me so much that he provided a way for me to establish this relationship with him and that was by Jesus Christ.

He explained that Jesus lived on earth for thirty-three years, and during that time he lived a perfect life. He never sinned. That was the reason Jesus is so important. God became man in the flesh, in the person of Jesus Christ, who was the only man who did not sin. So he qualified to assume my sins. As a businessman, I could understand that—it was like a home purchaser having to qualify before he could assume a mortgage. Christ qualified!

The only thing I had to do was ask Jesus into my life, and I did.

"Behold, I stand at the door and knock; if anyone hears my voice and opens the door, I will come into him."

Revelation 3:20, NASB

As my business associates will tell you, I am a very practical person—if something does not work, I quickly eliminate it. I can tell you from experience that a relationship with the living God is possible through Jesus Christ. Nothing I know of compares with the privilege of knowing Christ personally.

If you do not know whether you have this relationship, I encourage and challenge you to ask Christ into your life and settle this issue by repeating this simple prayer.

Lord Jesus, I need you. I open the door of my life and invite you in as my Savior and Lord. Thank you for forgiving my sins and giving me the gift of eternal life. Amen.

You might fulfill each of the principles in becoming a faithful steward, but without a relationship with Christ, you will never be content.

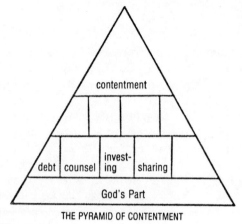

contentment

debt | counsel | invest-ing | sharing

God's Part

THE PYRAMID OF CONTENTMENT

NINE
SHARING—A POD OF PEAS

It is more blessed to give than to receive.

Acts 20:35

I will never forget a Sunday morning several years ago. It was time for the collection and, as usual, my stream of thought went something like this:

"I wonder if I'm obligated to give this week . . . I gave $5 last week."

"Churches are always asking for money. I bet most of them don't have any idea how to properly administer their budget."

"I better put something in the plate, even if it's just a dollar. I wouldn't want that couple next to me to think I'm stingy."

"I wonder what Mr. Johnson gives each week. He makes so much money. He looks like the type who doesn't give much."

"That TV program last night on the African famine was shocking. I really feel for those starving kids. Someday, when I can afford it, I'll try to help them out."

"Well, at least this dollar is a tax deduction."

After the collection, the pastor simply quoted one Scripture:

Let each one do just as he has purposed in his heart; not grudgingly or under compulsion; for God loves a cheerful giver.

2 Corinthians 9:7, NASB

Grudgingly or under compulsion. Grudgingly or under compulsion. The words kept running through my mind. That was my history of giving.

I had been a Christian for more than two years, and during that time I never had been a "cheerful giver." I knew I was supposed to be cheerful, and I gave the impression that I enjoyed sharing, but in my heart it was painful for me to part with my hard-earned money.

I occasionally would give to relieve my conscience, and at other times to impress others as to how "with it" I was spiritually. But I had never remotely approached giving with any enjoyment.

In fact, I would become very defensive at the mere mention of a collection. Part of the reason my attitude was so negative was the seemingly endless competition for my dollars among charitable organizations. Such campaigns are often conducted on a level that rivals Madison Avenue.

The biggest reason for my frustration in sharing was that I had not been taught the purposes and the practical "how to's" of sharing. Since being exposed to what Scripture says about sharing, the Holy Spirit has been changing my attitudes, and I have begun to experience the joy of sharing. Indeed, sharing has perhaps been the most liberating area of study in my Christian experience.

Without apology the Old and New Testaments place a great deal of emphasis on giving.

In fact, more verses have to do with sharing than any other subject on money. There are commands, practical suggestions, examples, and exhortations concerning this facet of stewardship. Everywhere in the Bible covetousness and greed are condemned, and generosity and charity are encouraged.

PURPOSE OF SHARING

The major purpose of sharing is to benefit the giver. Jesus said, "It is more blessed to give than to receive." It might be said that giving is not God's way of raising money, it's God's way of raising men. In fact, the Lord as owner of the cattle on a thousand hills has said he does not ever need our money—"If I [the Lord] were hungry, I would not mention it to you—for all the world is mine and everything in it" (Psalm 50:10).

Sharing benefits the giver in three primary areas: 1) in the development of a godly character, 2) in reaching our goal of contentment, and 3) in making truly lasting investments.

The Development of Character.   The Lord understands that for us to develop into the people he wants us to be, we must learn how to share our possessions freely. If we don't, our inbred selfishness will grow and dominate us.

"An extreme example is Howard Hughes. In his youth Hughes was a typical playboy, with a passion for parties and beautiful women and an aversion toward giving. As he grew older and turned an inheritance into a vast fortune, he became more and more closed-fisted. He let his wealth create an ever-increasing barrier between himself and other people. In his last years he lived in seclusion, becoming a recluse whose life was devoted to avoiding germs and people."[8]

In sharp contrast to Hughes was George Mueller who, like Hughes, inherited wealth, but established a lifelong pattern of generous sharing. His life was characterized by serving the needs of others. Sharing leads to life itself. It is the most effective antidote to the human disease of covetousness. "Instruct them to be generous and ready to share . . . so that they may take hold of that which is life indeed" (1 Timothy 6:18, 19, NASB).

Sharing Is Essential for Contentment.   A consistent habit of sharing is the best reminder that God is the sovereign owner of all we have been given to possess. As we share our money, this helps to sharpen our focus on the part that God plays, and God's part is the foundation of contentment.

Sharing also trains our attention on the living God. "It teaches us to put God first in our lives" (Deuteronomy 14:23). An effective way of helping to visualize God's involvement in our sharing is to imagine that you are placing your gift into the nail-scarred hands of the Lord Jesus himself.

Giving Is An Investment.   It is a tragic fact of history that people usually react rather than act. We wait until the problem is too large to avoid before we do something about it.

Dr. John R. Mott talked about this in 1905. "We in America have a choice," he said. "We can give from our abundance and make an investment by sending 1,000 missionaries to Japan, or within fifty years we will be forced to send 200,000 of our boys with guns and bayonets."

We responded by sending only six missionaries. However, Mott was not exactly correct in his prediction. It wasn't fifty years; it was thirty-six years. It was not 200,000 of our youth; it was a million. It was not just guns and bayonets—it was the atomic bomb.[9]

Will we as a people of plenty learn the lessons history offers to teach us? General MacArthur, addressing those who watched the signing of the Peace Treaty in 1945 aboard the U.S.S. *Missouri,* observed that the only way to prevent another such holocaust as World War II is by a "birth of the spirit."

In its efforts for peace the United States has invested billions in foreign countries. Our government's generous efforts have largely failed, resulting in disdain and hatred throughout the world. The compassionate sharing of wealth can ultimately be successful only when coupled with exposing people to the person of Jesus Christ.

Only through a relationship with Christ can the hearts of men be changed.

ETERNAL INVESTMENTS

Our Lord also wants us to know that whatever we share on earth becomes an eternal investment accruing to our account.

As Francis Schaeffer said, "We are often told, 'You can't take it with you.' But this is not true. You can take it with you—if you are a Christian.

"Jesus himself taught this:

Do not lay up for yourselves treasures upon earth where moth and rust destroy, and where thieves break in and steal; but lay upon yourselves treasures in heaven, where neither moth nor rust destroys, and where thieves do not break in or steal.

Matthew 6:19, 20, NASB

"This statement is to be taken literally. Jesus never uttered mere 'God-words.' We can lay up money in land and investments, but we can lay it up just as realistically and objectively in heaven."[10]

Jesus says it's as if the money given by faith in God is exchanged for eternal currency which is deposited in our account in the bank of heaven.

It is truly more blessed to give than to receive.

HOW MUCH DO WE SHARE?

Old Testament society was governed by law that strictly set the minimum amount to be given—the tithe, or a tenth of a person's earnings. When the children of Israel disobeyed this commandment, it was regarded as robbing God himself. Listen to Jehovah's solemn words in Malachi's days:

"You have robbed me of the tithes and offering due to me. And so the awesome curse of God is cursing you, for your whole nation has been robbing me."

Malachi 3:8, 9

In addition to the tithe, the Hebrews were encouraged to give offerings which were voluntary.

The New Testament builds on the foundation of the tithe and offering. The first addition is the instruction to give "as God has prospered you."

On every Lord's Day each of you should put aside something from what you have earned during the week, and use it for this offering. The amount depends on how much the Lord has helped you earn.
                                        1 Corinthians 16:2, NASB

Second, the New Testament encourages sacrificial giving:

Now I want to tell you what God in his grace has done for the churches in Macedonia. Though they have been going through much trouble and hard times, they have mixed their wonderful joy with their deep poverty, and the result has been an overflowing of giving to others. They gave not only what they could afford, but far more.
                                        2 Corinthians 8:1–3

Notice the great care taken to show that it was not in circumstances of prosperity that the Macedonians gave their liberal offering.

Frankly, in our affluent society the average person does not often find himself in a position where he is forced to share sacrificially. A family in our neighborhood fasts for a meal or a day each week and gives the money it saves in the cost of food as a practical way of experiencing giving from a personal sacrifice.

In Mark 12:43, 44, Jesus remarked, "That poor widow has given more than all those rich men put together! For they gave a little of their extra, while she gave up her last penny." It is obvious Jesus was not talking about amount; she gave the smallest denomination possible. In God's economy attitude is more important than the amount.

Nowhere is the importance of attitude stressed more than in 1 Corinthians 13:3: "If I give all my possessions to feed the poor . . . but do not have love, it profits me nothing" (NASB).

Bev and I have given a great deal of thought and prayer to the question of "how much" we should share. We have come to the conclusion that for us, the tithe is the minimum amount. Then, the more God prospers us, the greater percentage we should share from our income. I encourage you to prayerfully consider the amount God is calling you to share.

There are things I like about the tithe. It is a simple and systematic method of sharing. However, it has a potential trap that I sometimes find myself falling into—treating the tithe as just another bill to be paid, and not reflecting or praying about its use.

In fact, I believe that there is a reason why Scripture is unclear on exactly how much we should share. The decision as to the amount an individual gives should be based on a personal relationship with God. As he seeks the guidance of the Spirit through an active prayer life, sharing suddenly becomes an exciting adventure.

The Abernathy family is an example. They used to own a shoe store. The members of the family had been praying that God would direct their sharing. As they prayed, they were impressed with the needs of the Wilsons, a large family in their community.

Finances were tight for the Wilsons because the school year was starting. The Abernathys decided to give each of the five Wilson children two pairs of shoes. They did not know that the gift had been precisely what the Wilson children had been praying for.

Around the dinner table that evening as the Wilson children began to pray for the shoes, the mother said, "You don't have to ask the Lord for shoes anymore. God has heard your prayers and answered." One by one the shoes were brought out.

By the time it was over, the children thought God was in the shoe business!

I wish you could have seen the excitement and sense of

awe on the faces of the Abernathys as they experienced first-hand how God was directing their sharing through the quiet mystery of prayer.

WHOM DO WE GIVE TO?

We are told to share with three categories of people. With whom and in what proportion one shares varies with the needs God lays on the heart of each believer.

The Family.   In our culture we are experiencing a tragic breakdown in this area of sharing. Husbands have failed to provide for their wives, parents have neglected their children, and grown sons and daughters have forsaken their elderly parents. Such neglect is solemnly condemned.

If any one does not provide for his own, and especially for those of his household, he has denied the faith, and is worse than an unbeliever.
1 Timothy 5:8, NASB

Meeting the needs of your family and relatives is the first priority in giving and one in which there should be no compromise.

Christian Work and Workers.   Throughout its pages the Bible focuses on maintenance of the ministry. The Old Testament priesthood was to receive specific support (Numbers 18:21), and the New Testament teaching on ministerial support is just as strong. However, some have wrongly taught proverty for Christian workers. Thus many believe that those who are in various forms of Christian ministry should be poor. That position is not scriptural.

Pastors who do their work well should be paid well and should be highly appreciated, especially those who work hard at both preaching and teaching.
1 Timothy 5:17

How many Christian workers have been driven to distraction from their ministry by inadequate support? How many full-time Christian workers have had their dignity destroyed by having to accept handouts and "pastors' discounts" in order to make ends meet? God never intended his servants to exist at the level of bare subsistence. As someone has said, "The poor and starving pastor should exist only among poor and starving people."

People often ask Bev and me whether all our giving is done through our local church. In our case, the answer is no. A large portion of our giving supports our local church because we believe we should support the places that minister to our personal needs. The remainder of the support which we earmark for Christian work goes to ministries beyond our local church.

The Poor.   I didn't go to bed hungry last night—I never do. But conservative estimates are that one billion people in the world go to bed hungry each night. That kind of statistic is awesome. It gives us the feeling that there is nothing we can do about such an immense problem.

Christians are instructed to give to the poor. It is an important teaching that is emphasized by the fact that the poor and the destitute are mentioned in the majority of those verses that discuss who should be the recipient of our sharing. "If you give to the poor, your needs will be supplied. But a curse upon those who close their eyes to poverty" (Proverbs 28:27).

As Roger Palms observed, "Obviously there are no simple answers. We have no voice in what foreign national leaders do, especially those who allow their own people to go hungry in order to ship food to rich nations. I had always assumed that the rich nations were feeding the poorer nations, but most of the years since 1955 the U.S. has imported more food from hungry lands than it has exported to them."[11] We must be diligent and creative in determining how we can most effectively identify the poor throughout our own country and the world. Then we must work to meet their needs.

Our family has made personal contact with the poor

themselves and through ministries that are directly
involved in meeting the needs of the poor. This has helped
to make sharing more real to our family and has given us
the opportunity to evaluate how effectively our gifts are
being used.

THE PATTERN OF SHARING

During Paul's third missionary journey he wrote the
Corinthians concerning a promised collection to meet the
needs of the persecuted believers in Jerusalem.

*On the first day of every week let each one of you put aside
and save, as he may prosper, that no collections be made
when I come.*

1 Corinthians 16:2, NASB

His comments provide a practical method of sharing.
Let's call this pattern "Paul's Pod of Peas": Personal,
Periodic, Private Deposit, and Premeditated.

Personal is the first of Paul's Peas. Giving is
incumbent on each person. "Let each one of you . . . ." It is
the privilege and responsibility of every Christian, young
and old, rich and poor. Because God always associated the
gift with the giver, giving is a personal matter in which
every believer sustains a direct and individual
responsibility to the Lord.

Six years ago I met a neighbor in Orlando who left me
almost speechless because of the pleasure he experienced
from giving. I had never met a person like that before.
And as our relationship has grown I have discovered how
he established a pattern of joyful giving. His parents
shared liberally with those in need and required that each
of their children establish the habit of sharing from
childhood. As a consequence, he enjoys a level of freedom
in sharing that few people experience.

Periodic is the second of Paul's Peas. In the Old
Testament the tithe was usually collected annually, but in
the New Testament sharing was to be a weekly
contribution: " . . . upon the first day of the week . . . ." The

increased frequency for giving is God's remedy for our
irregularity and lack of discipline.

As a family we are coming to appreciate the wisdom of
a consistent time together to thank God for providing for
our needs and to discuss how we should channel our
giving. I sometimes neglect this process, and after such
times I more fully realize the importance of the family
gathering to make decisions on sharing and to praise him
for his consistent provision.

Private Deposit is the third of Paul's Peas. When Paul
wrote to the Corinthians he encouraged them to put their
funds in private deposit: ". . . Put aside and save . . . ."

We have tried to work this out practically by
establishing a separate checking account that we call the
"Lord's Account." After we decide how much to give to the
Lord, we deposit the money into the Lord's Account. It is
out of that account that we share. The balance in the
Lord's Account fluctuates as we set aside and save, and
then share to meet needs.

Probably the most gratifying part of setting aside
money has been the thrill of praying that God would
make us aware of needs to meet, and then being able to
answer someone's prayers who is in need.

Premeditated is the last in Paul's Pod of Peas. Almost
every Sunday after I became a Christian Bev would ask
me, "Honey, how much would you like to give this week
at church?" My standard reply was, "Whatever turns you
on."

Because of my disdainful and flippant attitude, I was
not in a position to experience the blessing meant for the
giver. To know the full joy and reap the blessing of
sharing, it must not be done carelessly.

*Let each one do just as he has purposed in his heart; not
grudgingly or under compulsion; for God loves a cheerful
giver.*

2 Corinthians 9:7, NASB

Sharing is to be a deliberate, premeditated act. It
should involve thought, planning, and prayer. However, I

suspect that many believers operate like I used to—never thinking about giving until it is time for the collection.

The supreme example of premeditated giving was set by our Savior, "who for the joy set before Him endured the cross" (Hebrews 12:2, NASB). Indeed, his sacrifice is a reminder that giving is at the very heart of the Christian faith. God so loved that he gave.

CONTRAST

Society says: It is more blessed to receive than to give.
Scripture says: "It is more blessed to give than to receive" (Acts 20:35).

COMMITMENT

Establish a time each week when you can gather as a family to discuss and pray about sharing. Use the time to review this chapter.

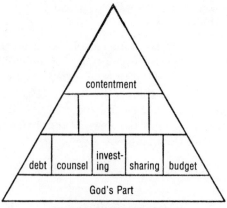

THE PYRAMID OF CONTENTMENT

TEN
BUDGET—KEEP ABREAST
OF THE FACTS

Annual income twenty pounds, Annual expenditure
nineteen nineteen six, Result happiness.
Annual income twenty pounds, Annual expenditure twenty
pounds ought and six, Result misery.

Charles Dickens

The day Bev and I went to see the Websters, they were
enjoying the visit of their first granddaughter, Heather.
As they watched her play, there was not even a hint of
what they had gone through the previous year.

For Frank and Vivian Webster it had been a year of
dramatic upheaval. Frank had suffered a stroke that
paralyzed his left side and resulted in the loss of his job.
They were forced to sell their cozy lake-front home and
readjust to a much lower standard of living.

The clean, neat apartment they now called home was
sparsely furnished. It was apparent that they were going
through hard times. Vivian explained their readjustment.
"We have been amazed at what we can live without. We
have been forced to watch every penny and follow a strict
budget."

Their backs were against a financial wall, and the Websters had responded by economizing at every turn: they went without air conditioning and TV and limited the use of the hot water heater to thirty minutes a day—just enough for showers and the dishes. Their conservation was paying off. Despite an increase in utilities, the monthly electric bill was averaging only $11.50. They were actually putting more money into savings than when they were living on Frank's lucrative salary as an engineer. However, during those years of easy spending, they had lived without the restraints of a budget.

"The trauma of unemployment forced us to communicate in an area of our lives that had been 'off limits' during the 'good old days,' " Vivian explained. "We have learned more about each other through this adversity than at any other time during our twenty-seven years of marriage. As strange as this may sound, we are grateful that this hardship happened. There is more peace in our family now than during the years of prosperity."

WHAT IS A BUDGET?

The Websters are proof that when a family plans where its money is to go, it can make the money go further. That's what a budget is—a plan for spending money.

Actually it is simple and easy when you understand its purpose, follow a workable plan, and use it to maximize your income.

WHY BUDGET?

Budgeting Makes Your Money Go Further.   When the bank notified the depositor of her overdraft she replied in disbelief, "I must have more money left in my account. I still have six checks in my checkbook!"

Like the surprised depositor, if you do not have a written budget chances are that you are flying by the seat of your financial pants.

Budgeting is not always fun, but it is the only way to follow through and apply what has been learned about getting out of debt, saving, and sharing and still meet basic needs. Regardless of the income, most families have difficulty making ends meet unless there is a plan for spending. As someone has said, "Expenses will always tend to rise just a little higher than income."

I have seen countless examples of this. Invariably, whether a family earns $8,000 or $80,000 a year, it probably will have too much month at the end of the money unless there is a carefully planned and disciplined approach to spending.

Using a budget introduces an attitude of control in spending that is needed to reach financial objectives.

Budgeting Provides an Opportunity to Work and Pray Through Spending Decisions as a Family.   This is important because 48 percent of the most serious marital problems are financial, according to a recent survey of young husbands. In fact, one judge has said, "Quarreling about money is the major reason for America's unprecedented divorce rate." I seldom see a family with financial problems where there is not real tension within the marriage.

A successful budget should be a "team effort." Budgeting can help each member of the family participate in deciding what should be purchased and what the goals of the family should be. It is a good tool for the husband and wife to use for communicating together.

A budget can also help a family get full value for its money without losing sight of the things its members want most. A family in our neighborhood is committed to sending their children to camp each summer for two weeks. Several years ago as they were planning their annual budget in January, it became apparent that there would not be enough money for the children to go to camp.

The family then agreed each member would "contribute" to summer camp by making a sacrifice: the father gave up his golf game once a month, the mother did not join her summer bowling league, and the children received no birthday presents. By using a budget, the family was able to anticipate a problem and make adjustments in their spending to enable the members to get what they wanted most—in this case, summer camp.

HOW TO BUDGET

No one I have known to be in financial difficulty used a budget. Some had made a budget and then promptly filed it away. Others had made an unrealistic budget that provided nothing for such items as clothing or medical care. A budget is useful only if it is used. It should be a plan tailor-made for managing *your* finances, not someone else's.

To set up your budget, you need only a simple inexpensive notebook of accounting paper that can be bought in most bookstores. Then follow these three steps:

Step 1—Where We Are Today.   Developing a budget must begin with the current situation. Determine precisely how much money is earned and spent.

In my experience spending tends to be significantly underestimated, particularly in the areas of food, clothing, transportation, and the "miscellaneous" expenses. For this reason it is essential for the family to keep a strict accounting of every penny for a month to get an accurate picture of what they are actually spending.

The most efficient way to accomplish this is to pay for all large purchases by check. Then, have each family member carry a small notebook or a three-by-five card to record all cash purchases. In the evening record the check and cash purchases under the appropriate category on the Monthly Budget Form.

The Monthly Budget Form below is a guide that you can alter to fit your situation.

MONTHLY BUDGET FORM

INCOME PER MONTH		EXPENSES PER MONTH	
Salary	_____	1. Sharing	_____
Interest income	_____	2. Taxes	
Dividends	_____	(b) Income taxes	_____
Rental income	_____	(b) Social	
Other income	_____	Security	_____
		(c) Other taxes	_____
Total Income	=======		
		3. Saving	_____
		4. Housing	
		(a) Payments	_____
		(b) Insurance	_____
		(c) Taxes	_____
		(d) Maintenance	_____
		(e) Telephone	_____
		(f) Utilities	_____
		(g) Other	_____
		5. Food	
		(a) Eating at home	_____
		(b) Eating out	_____
		6. Clothing	_____
		7. Transportation	
		(a) Payments	_____
		(b) Gasoline	_____
		(c) Maintenance	_____
		(d) Other	_____
		8. Insurance	
		(a) Automobile	_____
		(b) Life	_____
		(c) Health	_____
		9. Miscellaneous	
		(a) Medical/Health	_____
		(b) Education	_____
		(c) Gifts	_____
		(d) Vacations	_____
		(e) Recreation	_____
		(f) Personal allowance	_____
		(g) Other	_____
		10. Debt Reduction	
		(a) Credit card	_____
		(b) Installment	_____
		(c) Other	_____
		Total Expenses	=======

If your wages are not the same each month (like the income of a commissioned salesman), make a conservative estimate of your annual income and divide by twelve to determine your monthly income.

Then complete the Annual Expense Form for those expenses that do not occur each month. Examples are real estate taxes and homeowner's insurance which are paid annually. Divide the yearly premium by twelve to arrive at the monthly expense. This Annual Expense Form will also be helpful in reminding you when to anticipate these periodic expenses.

ANNUAL EXPENSE FORM 19__

ITEM	JAN	FEB	MAR	APR	MAY	JUN	JUL	AUG	SEP	OCT	NOV	DEC
real estate taxes											$300	
home owners insurance					$225							

Some expenses, such as vacations and auto repairs, do not come due every month. Estimate how much you spend for these on a yearly basis, divide that amount by twelve, and fill in the appropriate categories on the Monthly Budget Form.

Armed with this information you can construct an accurate budget of what you are actually spending and earning today. Do not be discouraged! Almost every budget I have seen starts out with expenditures in excess of income. But there is a solution.

Step 2—The Solution—Where We Want To Be.   To solve the problem of spending more than you earn, you must either increase your income to the level of your expenditures or decrease your expenditures to the level of your income.

It's that simple—either earn more or spend less. There are no other alternatives.

ADDING TO YOUR INCOME.   A part-time job, or better yet a family project that would involve the whole family, are ways of increasing your income. The ever-present danger of increasing income is the tendency for expenses also to rise. The key for eliminating this problem is to agree ahead of time to apply any extra income to balancing the budget.

Another potential problem is to sacrifice family relationships in order to earn extra money. Extra income is valuable only as it helps the family get more of what it wants out of life.

REDUCING EXPENSES.   My father was in the hotel business as I was growing up. He owned a resort in Florida that catered to tourists. Business was seasonal—during the winter it flourished, in the summer it practically withered and died.

He tells me that just the thought of summer sent chills down his spine, but after the lean months he was always grateful. Summer taught him the habit of asking these questions about his expenses: Which are absolutely necessary? Which can I do without? Which can I reduce?

You can ask these same questions of your personal budget as you work to reduce spending.

Here are some guidelines to help you evaluate your major expenses. When you exceed the upper range in any category, this should warn you to carefully evaluate your expenditures.

CATEGORY	PERCENT OF INCOME (after sharing and taxes)
Shelter	20–35%
Food	15–25%
Transportation	10–15%

Clothing	4– 8%
Insurance	3– 5%
Health	3– 5%
Entertainment & Recreation	3– 5%
Debts	0–10%
Saving	5–10%
Miscellaneous	3– 5%

The best way to reduce spending is to plan ahead. Decide in advance what you need and make a list. By using the "need list," you will be able to shop more wisely and avoid impulse spending. Consider these suggestions:

Shelter:

1) Purchase an older house that you can improve with your own labor, or buy a modest-size house suitable to your needs today with a design that can be expanded should you need more space in the future.

2) Consider apartment living. It is less expensive and without the responsibilities—lawn care, maintenance, etc.

3) If you can do repair and maintenance work such as lawn spraying, pest control, painting, and carpet cleaning, you will save a substantial amount.

4) Lower the cost of utilities by limiting the use of heating, air conditioning, lights, and appliances.

5) Shop carefully for furniture and appliances. Garage sales are a good source for reasonably priced household goods.

Food:

1) Prepare a menu for the week. Then list the ingredients from the menu and shop according to the list. This will help you plan a nutritionally balanced diet. Avoid impulse shopping, and eliminate waste.

2) Shop once a week. Each time we go shopping for "some little thing," we always buy "some other little thing" as well.

3) Cut out the ready-to-eat food which has expensive labor added to the price.

4) Leave children and hungry husbands home. The fewer distractions from the list the better.

5) The husband's lunches are often budget breakers. A lunch prepared at home and taken to work will help the budget and the waistline.

6) Reduce the use of paper products—paper plates, cups, and napkins are expensive to use.

Transportation:

1) If it is possible to get by with one car, this will be the biggest transportation savings.

2) Purchase a low-cost used car and drive it until repairs become too expensive.

3) The smaller the car, the more economical to operate. You pay an estimated 35¢ a pound each year to operate an automobile.

4) Perform routine maintenance yourself—oil changes, lubrication, etc. Regular maintenance will prolong the life of your car.

5) If purchasing a new car, wait until new models are introduced in September. You can save 5 to 35 percent during these year-end sales.

Clothing:

1) Make a written list of yearly clothing needs. Shop from the list during the off-season sales, at economical clothing stores and at garage sales.

2) A wife who uses a sewing machine can cut the cost of garments in half.

3) Purchase simple basic fashions that stay in style longer than faddish clothes.

4) Do not purchase a lot of clothing. Select one or two basic colors for your wardrobe, and buy outfits that you can wear in combination with others.

5) Purchase home-washable fabrics. Clothes that must be commercially cleaned are expensive to maintain.

Insurance:

1) Select insurance based on your *need* and budget, and secure estimates from three major insurance companies.

2) Exercising the deductible feature will substantially reduce premiums.

3) Seek the recommendation of friends for a skilled insurance agent. A good agent can save you money.

Health:

1) Practice preventive medicine. Your body will stay healthier when you get the proper amount of sleep, exercise, and nutrition.

2) Also practice proper oral hygiene for healthy teeth and to reduce dental bills.

3) Obtain the recommendation of friends for reasonable and competent physicians and dentists.

Entertainment and Recreation:

1) Time your vacation for the off-season and select destinations near home.

2) Rather than expensive entertainment, seek creative alternatives such as family picnics or exploring free state parks.

FIVE BUDGETING HINTS.

1) Reconcile your checkbook each month.

2) It is helpful to have a special savings account, in which to put aside the monthly allotment for the bills that do not come due each month. For example, if your annual insurance premium is $240, each month deposit twenty dollars in this savings account. This method will insure that the money will be available when these payments come due.

3) We are trained to think monthly. To better understand the impact of an expense, extend it to a yearly cost. For example, if the husband spends $2.50 for lunch each working day, multiply $2.50 by five days a week by fifty-two weeks a year. It totals $650 for lunches. This will help you give proper attention to the seemingly inconsequential expenses.

4) Control impulse-spending. Impulse-spending ranges from buying automobiles to snacks. Here is a suggestion on how to control such spending. Each time you have the urge to spend for something not planned, post it to an "impulse list" and date it. Then wait thirty days and pray about buying the item. If you're like me, I guarantee that you will not purchase at least half of the items, because impulses do not last. If you don't believe me, just look at the garage sales in your neighborhood.

5) It is wise for the husband and wife to include personal allowances in the budget. Each should be given an allowance to spend as they please. The wife can go to the beauty shop and the husband can play golf as often as they like, so long as the allowance holds out. This will eliminate many arguments.

Step 3—Do Not Stop!   The most common temptation is to stop budgeting. Don't do it!

Remember, a budget is simply a plan for spending your money. It will not work by itself. Every area of your budget should be regularly reviewed to keep a rein on spending. "Any enterprise is built by wise planning, becomes strong through common sense, and profits wonderfully by keeping abreast of the facts" (Proverbs 24:3, 4).

To help us "keep abreast of the facts," at the middle of each month Bev and I compare our actual income and expenses with the amounts budgeted. If we find ourselves overspending, we make mid-month adjustments by cutting back on our spending plans for the rest of the month. You need to maintain adequate records to compare the money actually spent with your budget.

Through the years there will be frustrations, but a budget, if properly used, will save you thousands of dollars. It will help you accumulate the savings for your children's education and your retirement. It will help you stay out of debt. More important, it will help the husband and wife communicate together in an area that is a leading cause of marital conflict.

COMMITMENT

Keep a strict accounting of all expenditures for thirty days to determine your current situation. After that, plan a budget suited to your income and personal objectives. Finally, use it.

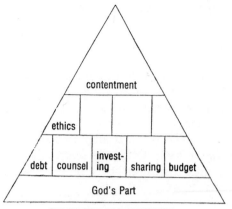

THE PYRAMID OF CONTENTMENT

ELEVEN
ETHICS—ABSOLUTELY

*Everyone did whatever he wanted to—whatever seemed
right in his own eyes.*

Judges 17:6

On a clear day the view is breath-taking from United
Brands Company corporate headquarters on the 44th floor
of the Pan Am Building in mid-Manhattan. Majestically
tall office buildings form a canyon of Park Avenue.

It was in an office overlooking this vista that Eli M.
Black, chairman of United Brands, worked as many as
sixteen to eighteen hours a day. From this office he guided
his $2 billion multi-national company through a tight
financial squeeze during a disaster-plagued 1974.

On February 3, 1975, from every business point of
view the worst was behind Eli Black. At 8:20 that gray
Monday morning, the fifty-three-year-old executive locked
his office doors, smashed his attache case through his
office window, and jumped to his death. He left no suicide
note, no word to explain his death.

Eli Black's death raised questions about the man.
Moreover, the event again raised a significant question
about the business world. Can a man with high moral
standards survive in an uncompromising financial world
that demands steadily increasing earnings?

Eli Black was a tenth-generation Rabbi. When he could not reconcile the strong ethical standard of his Rabbinic training with the "end justifies the means" standard of the business world, he apparently saw no alternative but to take his life.

Like Eli Black, all of us—the executive, the employee, and the housewife—are constantly tempted to bend the truth in our own favor. Often we know what we should do but find it is difficult to resist what "everybody else" is doing.

ETHICAL FOUNDATION

Obviously, we all need guidelines for doing what is right. The Bible offers a foundation for making ethical decisions. The cornerstone of this foundation can be found in the Ten Commandments in general, and two in particular:

You must not steal.

Exodus 20:15

You must not be envious of your neighbor's house, or want to sleep with his wife, or want to own his slaves, oxen, donkeys, or anything else he has.

Exodus 20:17

In Exodus 21, 22, and 23, Moses elaborated on the Commandments by developing the laws of liability, restitution, and justice. The law for Old Testament society governed business ethics and relationships. It required integrity, ensuring a person he could depend upon those with whom he was dealing.

In the New Testament Jesus adds another dimension. He establishes an ethic that does not exclusively preoccupy itself with the legality of an act. It also considers the motive and the impact on others. For example, it might be perfectly legal for you to sell your home without disclosing a hidden problem to an unsuspecting purchaser. However, your Christian ethic would require you to tell the prospective buyer about the problem because *people,* in God's sight, are more important than *things.*

If you love your neighbor as much as you love yourself you will not want to harm or cheat him, or kill him or steal from him. And you won't sin with his wife or want what is his, or do anything else the Ten Commandments say is wrong. All ten are wrapped up in this one, to love your neighbor as you love yourself. Love does no wrong to anyone.

Romans 13:9, 10

SOCIETY'S RELATIVE ETHICS

Byron was reading the morning paper while his wife, Peggy, prepared breakfast. "Well, would you look at this. Another politician got caught with his hand in the cookie jar," he said. "I'll bet there isn't an honest bureaucrat in the entire country. What a bunch of crooks!"

But a few moments later Byron was smirking as he told Peggy how he planned to pad his expense account in such a way that he would get more money from his employer than he was entitled to receive.

Byron was not aware of the incongruity between his own behavior and his disgust of dishonesty in others. As he told Peggy, "The way inflation and taxes are going, you've got to be shrewd just to survive. The company doesn't need it. Besides, everyone does it."

The Bible speaks of relative ethics during a turbulent period of Israel's history in Judges 17:6: "Everyone did whatever he wanted to—whatever seemed right in his own eyes."

And that is where our society is today.

While you may think that that box of paper clips or that handful of pencils that you take home from the office are minor items, statistics on employee theft reveal that establishment of a dishonest pattern can grow like cancer.

1) U.S. employee theft amounted to $18 billion in 1977, according to the Commerce Department. A decade earlier it was an estimated $3 billion.

2) Employee theft is growing by about 20 percent a year.

3) Within five years it is estimated employees in the U.S. will be stealing $1 billion a week from their employers.

ABSOLUTE ETHICS

While our society may tolerate such behavior, our Christian heritage is persistent in its demand for ethical behavior in even the smallest matters.

For unless you are honest in small matters, you won't be in large ones. If you cheat even a little, you won't be honest with greater responsibilities.

Luke 16:10

A faithful steward is called to be honest in even the smallest details because a small sin is just as corrosive to the development of our character as a larger sin.

Even as I am writing, I think of the many areas in which I am failing in the ethical standard that God calls us to have—the unreturned neighbor's tool, failure to turn off the light to conserve electricity for my landlord, and that "harmless white lie" today at the office. We should be intolerant of anything unethical. This is a far cry from the standards of our contemporary culture in which the quest for tolerance has resulted in ambiguous and relative ethics.

Make no mistake, to be ethical is a tough struggle, but it is necessary if we really want to become faithful stewards.

GOD WILL NOT TOLERATE DISHONESTY

A very wealthy businessman moved to a neighboring town. His annual income approached $1 million a year, he traveled in chauffeur-driven limousines, and his assets were immense.

His business was understood to be dedicated to the

Lord. This gave many people the confidence to invest their life savings in his business.

Unfortunately, his business practices were unethical. Through a series of unforeseen financial reverses, coupled with his extravagant standard of living, he lost all that he had accumulated.

It is my conviction that eventually God will take away anything we acquire through dishonesty. "And if you are not faithful with other people's money, why should you be entrusted with money of your own?" (Luke 16:12).

When we are unethical, we are really saying that God is not God. We are acting as if God is not able to provide exactly what we need. We are trying to do God's part.

We are also saying that God is not capable of discovering our dishonesty and not powerful enough to discipline us.

I am grateful that God loves us enough to not tolerate our dishonesty. He knows that, left unpunished, it would destroy our character and our relationship with him.

Richard Halverson summed it up this way, "Someone has described unethical behavior as a shortcut. Stealing is a shortcut to work.

"Hardly a day goes by but a man is tempted to take some shortcut in his life and business. And at first glance it looks like the shortcut would pay off. It may pay off—with some quick and transient satisfaction—but in the long run it turns to ashes!

"At first his decision may look foolish in the light of observable data—but the wise man has mastered the art of taking into consideration certain other facts which are just as valid—even though invisible. The greatest fact to count on is God! And the man who does is the man who wins ultimately. He's basing his life on the bedrock of reality.

"Trouble comes when a man leaves God out of the consideration. He takes the shortcut. Even though there may be nothing tremendous at stake, he's been unfaithful and violated his own integrity.

"Had he taken God into his calculations he would have known the only intelligent course was God's way. No man can fail when he's on God's side! It may look like he is along the way—but at the finish—the balance is clearly in the favor of the man who takes God seriously! And until the outcome is final, he's able to live with himself because the peace of God rules in his life!"[12]

CONTRAST

Society says: The end justifies the means and everybody has a price.

Scripture says: "If you cheat even a little, you won't be honest with greater responsibilities" (Luke 16:10).

COMMITMENT

Prayerfully review this ethics checklist:

1. Do I report all income on my tax returns and are all my expenses legitimate?

2. Do I care for the property of others as if it were my own?

3. Do I have the habit of telling "little white lies"?

4. Do I ever misappropriate office supplies, stamps, or anything else of my employers?

5. If I am undercharged on a purchase, do I report it?

6. When dealing with others, do I look out for their interests as well as my own?

Ask God to show you any other unethical behavior, especially in the gray areas, that should be changed. This is an excellent area for you to have a counselor who can help encourage you and hold you accountable.

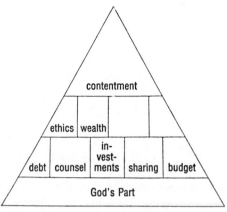

THE PYRAMID OF CONTENTMENT

TWELVE
WEALTH—REAL LIFE
AND REAL LIVING

*The futility of riches is stated very plainly in two places:
the Bible and the income tax form.*

*Happiness is not based on money, and the best proof of that
is our family.*

Christina Onassis

*He who loves money shall never have enough. The
foolishness of thinking that wealth brings happiness!*

Ecclesiastes 5:10

A young Roger Morgan came out of the Appalachian
Mountains in his early manhood with the firm purpose of
making a fortune. Money became his god and putting it
first, he became worth millions. Then the crash and the
Great Depression came, and he was reduced to utter
poverty.

Penniless, he took to the road. One day a fellow hobo
found him on the Golden Gate Bridge staring down into
the waters of the Bay, and he suggested they move on.

"Leave me alone," Roger replied. "I'm trying to think.
There is something more important than money, but I've
forgotten what it is."

What Roger Morgan forgot, or perhaps never knew, was the scriptural perspective of wealth and prosperity. It is essential for the faithful steward to understand three major aspects of this perspective:

Money Will Not Bring True Happiness in Life.   "Solomon, the author of Ecclesiastes, had an annual income of more than $25 million. He lived in a palace that took thirteen years to build. He owned 40,000 stalls of horses. He sat on an ivory throne overlaid with gold. He drank from gold cups. The daily menu of his household included a hundred sheep and thirty oxen in addition to fallow-deer and fatted fowl."[13]

Obviously, Solomon was in a position to know whether money would bring happiness, and he did not hesitate to say that riches do not bring true happiness:

He who loves money shall never have enough. The foolishness of thinking that wealth brings happiness! The more you have the more you spend, right up to the limits of your income.

Ecclesiastes 5:10, 11

In contrast, most Americans believe you can buy happiness. The American Institute of Public Opinion recently found that 70 percent of Americans thought they would be happier if they could earn only $37 more a week. I find myself periodically siding with this majority— falling into the "if only" trap.

"If only" I had a new car, I would be satisfied. "If only" I lived in that nice house, I would be content. "If only" I had his job, I would be happy. The list is endless.

This is a pattern that has been part of my life for as long as I can remember. Now that I am a Christian, I find myself adding a spiritual twist. I call it "if only . . . for the Lord." "If only" I made more money, then I would be able to give more to the Lord. "If only" I had his job, then I would be able to introduce more people to Christ. This issue is still a struggle in my life, although thanks be to God, it is becoming less frequent.

God has been patiently and lovingly steering me away from this pattern. I say lovingly, because God took the biggest area of personal weakness in my life, money and possessions, gave me the desire to start on this study, and then surrounded me with people who encouraged me to complete the seminar and this book. This consistent exposure to Scripture has been changing my attitudes and materialistic tendencies.

The Bible offers a sharp contrast to the attitude of the materialist. As someone has said,

Money will buy:
A bed but not sleep;
Books but not brains;
Food but not an appetite;
A house but not a home;
Medicine but not health;
Luxuries but not culture;
Amusement but not happiness;
A crucifix but not a Saviour.

Wealth is morally neutral, but dangerous. Many have misquoted 1 Timothy 6:10 to read that "money is the root of all evil." But money can be used for good or for evil. It can build hospitals and schools as well as finance hard drugs and war.

The root of all evil is in the mind of man, not his money. Sinfulness is determined by attitude, not affluence. Wealth will not corrupt a man if he has the proper perspective of it.

Scripture focuses on many men who were both wealthy and godly. Such men as Job, Abraham, Joseph, David, Daniel, and Joseph of Arimathaea are evidence that a person can be rich and still maintain a close relationship with God.

Nevertheless, hundreds of verses in Scripture warn of the dangers of wealth. The Lord wanted to make us aware of the ease with which we can trust in tangible wealth rather than the invisible, living God.

Jesus warned, "No servant can serve two masters; for either he will hate the one, and love the other, or else he will hold to one, and despise the other. You cannot serve God and riches" (Luke 16:13, NASB).

Haddon W. Robinson observes, "Serving money is very abstract. My house, my car, my investments do not mean more to me than God. But Jesus did *not* say that we must

serve God *more* than money. Evaluating our lives to
discover what occupies first place is not the proper test.
The question is whether we serve money at all.

"Either we serve God and use money or we serve
money and use God. Yet, few Christians deliberately
dedicate their lives to materialism. Wealth is deceitful,
Jesus told us, and its bondage is subtle. Like the flypaper
and the fly, the fly lands on the sticky substance thinking
'my flypaper' only to discover that the flypaper says 'my
fly.' "[14]

I have wrestled with this during my business career.
I was caught up in the excitement of building a new
business and unwittingly began to evaluate people in
terms of what they could do for me—not their worth as
people.

I found myself thinking more highly of those who were
wealthy or in a position to help me. However, I was
confronted with my attitude when I read James 1:4:
"Judging a man by his wealth shows you are guided by
the wrong motives." Without realizing it, I had been
caught by the deceitfulness of wealth. To avoid this trap,
we need to consistently evaluate our motives in light of
Scripture.

Wealth and Success.   According to Scripture, success in
finances is achieved by being a faithful steward. This is
obviously not the standard of success used by most people.
Usually the more wealth a person has accumulated, the
more he has been thought to "succeed." The more
expensive the home, the car, and the clothes, the more
successful he is considered to be. Such an attitude is
evidence that our success is related to how much we have.

However, according to Scripture it is impossible to tell
if a person is truly "successful" by looking at his external
circumstances, his possessions, or his position. If we had
seen Joseph or Paul in prison, Daniel in the lions' den, or
Job in his affliction and poverty—men who had lost
everything—how many of us would have considered them
successful?

Webster's definition of success is: "the degree or
measure of attaining a desired end." And according to

Scripture the desired end for us is to become faithful stewards. Then after we have fulfilled our responsibility by becoming faithful stewards (our part), it is up to God to decide whether or not to give us wealth (God's part). "Enjoy prosperity whenever you can, and when hard times strike realize that God gives one as well as the other" (Ecclesiastes 7:14).

So, as long as you are a faithful steward you can be content, whether you are struggling at the subsistence level or are fabulously wealthy. In other words, our part is to be faithful and God's part is to decide at what level of prosperity he wants us to live.

CONTRAST

Society says: "Wealth is instrumental in achieving happiness. It should be accumulated for financial security. The mark of a successful person is a healthy financial statement."

Scripture says: Wealth is no determiner of happiness. Our security is in the living God, not our possessions. The mark of a successful person is faithfulness.

COMMITMENT

Complete this Attitude Test to help you to determine whether you have the proper perspective on money.

1. Am I willing to sacrifice my family, reputation, clear conscience, and relationship with God or other people in order to acquire money?

2. Do I think more highly of people who are wealthy?

3. Am I critical of people who are wealthy?

4. What worries me?

5. What do I think about when my mind goes into neutral?

6. Do I trust in my money to do only what God can do?

7. Do I think "if only" I had more money, a larger home, a newer car, or a better job, then I would be happy?

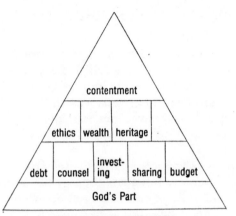

THE PYRAMID OF CONTENTMENT

THIRTEEN
LEAVING A HERITAGE—
THE ABC'S OF MONEY

Learning to handle money one step at a time is part of a child's education, a part which parents cannot leave to teachers but must direct themselves. Spending experiences are found in the outside world rather than in the classroom.

Train up a child in the way he should go, even when he is old he will not depart from it.

Proverbs 22:6, NASB

All of us are concerned about money—how to make it, how to save it, and how to spend it. However, we seldom think about how our values and habits shape our children's lives. Make no mistake, our parental attitudes toward money and patterns of spending deeply influence them.

A good example is George Bradbury, Jr., a young man in his mid-thirties who came to me for help. Julie, his wife, insisted he seek help or she would divorce him.

He did not seem to be a likely candidate for marital problems. He was personable and bright, and a college graduate with honors. Unfortunately, he was hopelessly immature when it came to handling money.

His problem began with a father who started with

nothing and built a multi-million dollar textile conglomerate. From a deprived family that struggled for existence, George Sr. grew up with a resolve that when he had a family of his own, things would be different.

True to his vow, nothing was too good or too much for "Little George." Little George was treated to an abundance of toys, exclusive camps, private boarding schools, a European sports car upon graduation, and much, much more.

"Big George" felt proud to know that he could satisfy his son's every desire and protect him from the harsh life that he had experienced.

But fortunes can change quickly. Foreign textile competition and a bitter union strike forced bankruptcy of the company.

Little George was unprepared for the turn of events. He was not able to last more than a year at any job, yet his free-spending habits continued unchecked. He was unable to cope with financial limitations.

Similarly, the majority of our younger people are learning to be undisciplined in handling their money. Their parents have neglected to train them in wise money management.

This is not the way things ought to be. Christian parents have an obligation to teach their children the biblical perspective concerning money and how to be faithful stewards.

Such education requires two steps:

First, parents themselves must know biblical financial principles and model them. For a moment, examine your attitudes toward money and your spending patterns. Can you see how you unconsciously "caught" many of your values and habits from your parents?

By far the most important way we can influence our children is by being a good model, because a great deal of a child's learning takes place by imitation. He learns to talk by imitating sounds he hears others make, and to walk by watching adults and attempting to copy their movements. Similarly, most of our children's attitudes about money are learned by unconsciously imitating those values and patterns held by their parents.

Second, parents must actively train their children to handle money based on principles taught in the Bible. There are not any hard and fast rules, but let's develop some guidelines for leaving your child a financial heritage. We'll discuss two areas:

1) Money Managing—the art of wise spending.
2) Money Making—the value of work.

The objective is to teach biblical principles to your children and then to prepare practical opportunities for them to experience the "working out" of these principles.

Of course the training must be geared to a child's age and learning ability.

LEARNING MONEY MANAGEMENT

Wise money management has to be learned, and it takes time and experience to acquire the art of wise spending. Therefore, learning to handle money one step at a time should be part of a child's education—a part which parents must direct themselves and not delegate to teachers, because spending experiences are found outside the schoolroom.

Before you try to teach your child how to manage money, you need to realize that a child is going to learn the art of money management only by actually managing money. Consider four areas where this is possible:

Allowances.   A primary means of teaching children the responsibilities of handling money is to give them an allowance. This should be done as soon as a child is ready for school.

The philosophy behind the allowance is two-fold. As a family member: 1) The child is entitled to a certain amount each week as his share of the family income; 2) He is responsible for routine chores without pay as his share of the family work—washing the dishes, etc.

The amount of the allowance will vary, of course, according to such factors as the child's age, his financial needs, and the financial circumstances of the family.

However, the amount of the allowance is not as

important as the responsibility of handling money. It is a
new experience, and the child will make many mistakes.
Don't hesitate to let the "law of natural consequences" run
its course. You're going to be tempted to help little
Johnny when he gets his quarter and spends it all the
first day on candy. You won't like the fact that he has to
live the rest of the week without all the other things he
wants and maybe needs. Don't bail him out. His mistakes
will be his best teacher.

Parents should offer advice on how to spend money,
but your child must have the responsibility of freedom of
choice. Excess restrictions will only reduce his
opportunities to learn by experience.

The first few pennies and nickels will make a lasting
impression. Every Saturday morning I used to walk to the
corner store with my son Matthew to buy him a "special
treat," a pack of his favorite gum. Despite my persistent
advice, the entire pack would be consumed that first day.

When we started to give him an allowance, we decided
that Matthew would have to buy his own gum. I will
never forget the pained look on his face as he came out of
the store with his first purchase that cost him two weeks
allowance. "Daddy, this gum costed me all my money!" he
blurted. That pack was rationed with tender care and
lasted more than a week.

Parents should slowly increase the allowance as the
child grows in his ability to handle additional purchases.
The father of a close friend used to periodically test his
three children. He would give each child money for their
clothes. If they were conscientious in the spending of the
money, shopping for the best values, the father knew they
were prepared for greater responsibilities and a larger
allowance. But if any of the children would spend the
money frivolously, the father knew that child needed to
mature before his allowance was increased.

Learning How to Budget.   When children begin to receive
an allowance, it will be an appropriate time to teach them
how to budget. Begin with a simple system consisting of
three boxes each labeled by category—save, spend, and

share. As you hand out the allowance each week, the child distributes a portion into each box. Thus, a simple budget is established using visual control. Even a six-year-old can understand this method because when there is no more money to spend, the box is empty.

By the time a child is nine or ten, he is old enough to be exposed to the family's budget and have a part in influencing budget decisions. This will be exciting for the child. He will understand that he is growing up because he can share in making plans for spending the family income. He will begin to realize that each member has a responsibility for thoughtful spending regardless of who provides the income. It will help him to realize the extent and limitations of the family income, and how to make the money stretch to meet the family's needs.

At first the child will often think that the family has so much money that it is impossible to spend it all. To help him visualize the budget, have the family income converted to a sack of half-dollars. Pour these on the table during family budget time and divide the "income" pile into the various "expense" piles representing the categories of family spending. It is often difficult for children to understand numbers because they are abstract. So the coins will be a tangible way for them to grasp the family budget.

In training your children how to budget, the goal should be to gradually increase their responsibility until they are independent in money management. See the "Strategy for Independence" section at the end of this chapter for guidelines on what levels of responsibilities children might be expected to assume at various ages.

Learning Saving and Investing. The discipline of saving should be established as soon as the child begins to receive an allowance. It is helpful to establish a savings account in the child's name as early as he can begin to understand earning interest. As he matures he should also be exposed to various types of investments: stocks, bonds, real estate, etc.

Moreover, it is appropriate to teach the cost of money and how difficult it is to get out of debt. Dick Getty told the story of loaning his son and daughter the money to buy bicycles. Dick drew up a credit agreement with a schedule for repayment of the loan including the interest charged. After they successfully went through the long, difficult process of paying off the loan, the family celebrated with a "mortgage burning" ceremony and a family picnic. Dick said that his children have appreciated those bikes more than any of their other possessions, and they have vowed to avoid debt in the future.

Learning to Share.   The best time to establish the personal habit of sharing is when you are young. Dr. Richard Halverson, pastor of Fourth Presbyterian Church in Washington, D.C., gave his son Chris this rich heritage as a child. Through World Vision, Chris and his brother gave money to support Kim, a Korean orphan who had lost his sight and an arm during the Korean War. Chris was taught to feel that Kim was his adopted brother. One Christmas, Chris bought Kim a harmonica. It was the first personal possession Kim had owned. He cherished this gift from his brother and learned to play it well.

Today, as an evangelist his presentation of the gospel includes his playing the harmonica. By being trained to share as a youth, Chris experienced firsthand the value of meeting people's needs and seeing God change lives as a result of faithfully sharing.

LEARNING HOW TO WORK

Work is an essential element in becoming a faithful steward. Thus parents have the responsibility to train children in the value and skills of work. If the child responds and learns how to work with the proper attitude, then he will not only have taken a giant step in becoming content, but he will become a valuable commodity in the job market. Good employees are difficult to find. Clearly, it is important for children to learn the dignity and habit of work. To

do this, careful planning and a definite program are
essential.

There are four areas to consider.

Expose Your Children to Your Work.   Not too many years
ago most children were active participants in earning the
family's money. They readily learned responsibility and
the value of money. However, that is seldom the case
today. It amazes me to find many children totally
unaware of how their fathers or mothers earn the family
income.

During a seminar several years ago, a participant said
that he had asked his father what he did at work. "I make
money," the father responded. "For a long time I thought
my dad actually made dollar bills. My mother also asked
Dad, 'How much did you draw this week?' I thought he
was really special to be able to do all that detailed
lettering and art work."

An important way to teach the value of work is to
expose the child to the parents' means of making a living.
If your children cannot visit you at work, at least take the
time to explain your job to them. For those parents who
manage their own business, children should be encouraged
to actively participate.

Learning Routine Responsibilities.   The best way for a
child to become a faithful steward in work is to establish a
habit of doing daily household chores.

These are unpaid chores that each member of the
family is expected to perform. For example, I never get
paid for carrying out the garbage, and my wife and son do
not get paid for doing the dishes. These chores should be
rotated for variety.

Earning Extra Money.   You should encourage your child
to do extra work to earn money. A good rule of thumb is
to pay the child a fair wage for the work you would have
to hire someone to do. For example, if your car needs
washing and your son needs some extra money and wants
to wash it, let him. Be happy to pay him rather than the
man at the car wash.

Encourage Your Child to Get a Job Working for Other People.   A paper route, baby sitting, janitorial work, or waiting on tables will be an education. A job gives a child a chance to enter into an employee-employer relationship and to earn extra money.

As your child enters high school it is a good idea to discontinue allowances during summer vacation. This will motivate him to earn his own money by holding a summer job. In fact, some students can handle part-time work during the school year. However, if your child is not one of these, encourage him to devote full time to his studies.

The objective of training your child in the value of work is to build and discipline his character. A working child with the proper attitude will be a more satisfied individual. He will grow up with more respect for the value of money and what goes into earning it.

OVERINDULGENCE

When it comes to money, parents are always on a tightrope trying to keep a proper balance. They can easily be too miserly with money, but in our affluent culture more often they are overindulgent and hamper the development of their child's character.

How many of us know of a father who once sold newspapers to earn a bicycle and now has a teen-age son who drives a sports car?

Clearly, overindulgence with money is destructive. It destroys the need for initiative and motivation. It creates a tendency to expect to be given things without giving anything in return.

STRATEGY FOR INDEPENDENCE

Lyle and Marge Nelsen of Orlando have four of the most mature and responsible children I have met. Their strategy has been to work toward having each child independently managing all of his own finances (with the exception of food and shelter) by the senior year in high school.

In this way they could be available to advise and counsel the children as they formed their spending philosophy and learned to make spending decisions. I think there is wisdom in this strategy.

Here are some broad guidelines on what responsibilities children in various age brackets might be expected to perform. The goal is independent management of money by the last year of high school. Remember each child is unique, and these are only suggested as a rough guide.

UNDER 6

Allowance: Use to pay for small items such as toys, books, and playthings.

Budget: Use the three box system (share, save, spend).

Saving: Open a savings account in the child's name and make a monthly deposit.

Work: Do routine household chores and be exposed to the parents' job.

AGES 6–9

Allowance: Use to pay for school lunches, school supplies, some recreation and hobbies, and gifts for others.

Budget: Continue to use the three box method supplemented with a simple written budget.

Sharing: Expand the child's vision in sharing to a situation that the child can personally know about.

Saving: Give the child an incentive to save for a bike or some other item that will require persistent saving.

Work: Begin to pay the child for some extra jobs around the home.

AGES 9–16

Allowance: Use to pay for all the above plus sports equipment, special events, and some clothing.

Budget: Use a more sophisticated written budget in conjunction with the boxes.

Saving: Encourage the child to begin to save for
          future transportation, or educational needs.
Work: The child can begin to work for other
          people by babysitting, cutting lawns, etc.
Sharing: Encourage the child to share with a
          foreign mission that he can learn about
          through personal contact.

AGES 16–18

Allowance: Use to pay for all clothing, grooming,
            school activities, transportation needs,
            and recreation.
Budget: Use a written budget with a checking
            account.
Sharing: Encourage the child to take on a local
            project in which he can become involved.
Saving: Save for his educational needs and for the
            future "nest egg." Expose the child to
            various types of investments and loans.
Work: Begin full-time summer employment and
            part-time or weekend employment during
            the school year.

CONTRAST

Society says: Do not require your children to establish the
discipline of managing money or of working hard.

Scripture says: Parents have the obligation of training
a child to be a faithful steward and wise money manager.

COMMITMENT

Husband and wife should evaluate what their children are
learning about handling money and work. Establish a
program to train your children to become faithful
stewards.

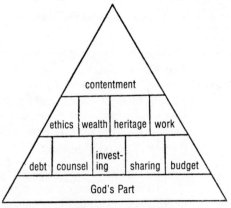

THE PYRAMID OF CONTENTMENT

FOURTEEN
WORK—IN PURSUIT
OF EXCELLENCE

Sloth, like rust, consumes faster than labor wears.

Benjamin Franklin

Diligence is the mother of good fortune.

Cervantes

*Whatever you do, do your work heartily, as for the Lord
rather than for men.*

Colossians 3:23, NASB

At age twenty-nine Allen Hitchcock felt trapped. For six
years he had worked as a clerk in a large department
store.

He was competent, and the job paid moderately well.
But as he looked around, he saw that those who were
promoted to management positions had college educations.
He longed for a future in management.

So, by taking night courses he completed college and
earned a degree in business administration. With his
degree the company soon promoted Allen to assistant
manager at a much higher salary.

The first few years were just as he had imagined—
reasonable hours, good wages, and attractive fringe
benefits. Then the unexpected happened.

The company expanded to Florida and the Hitchcocks were transferred. The expansion schedule called for strict deadlines, and Allen had major responsibilities.

At first he enjoyed the excitement of the challenge. However, soon his five-day week became six, and his normal eight-hour day stretched to fourteen hours. On top of that, his new supervisor was so demanding that Allen began to experience real tension at work.

He now had more work and more responsibility, but he no longer could earn overtime. So he made the same pay. As a result, resentment toward his employer was building. Allen began to wonder if management was worth the pressure.

Allen's job frustrations are not isolated. Few people are completely satisfied with their jobs. Boredom, lack of fulfillment, fear of losing their job, inadequate wages, overwork, and countless other pressures result in a high level of discontentment. Doctors, housewives, secretaries, salesmen, blue collar workers, and managers—regardless of the profession the frustrations are the same.

The average person in a fifty-year workspan spends 100,000 hours working. Most of an adult's life is involved in work, but usually with the job comes dissatisfaction. Perhaps no statistic shows the discontentment of Americans more than their job-hopping tendencies. A recent survey shows that the average American man changes jobs every four and one-half years, the average woman every three years.

Many just endure their work while ignoring the fact that 25 percent of their lifetime is devoted to a job which is distasteful. On the other hand, some people like work too much and neglect the other priorities of life.

People usually lean to one of two extremes: they either work as little as possible because work is unpleasant; or they tend to work all the time because it becomes overwhelmingly important.

However, Scripture teaches a balance in working. It affirms the value of work, but we are not to overwork. Work is designed to develop our character and to be the path to experiencing a more intimate relationship with the

Lord and with other people, as well as provide for our
material well-being.

In order for us to maintain a balance between working
too much or too little, and to find satisfaction in our work,
we need to understand what Scripture teaches about work.
The responsibilities of work are clearly divided between
our part and God's part.

OUR PART IN WORK

Five principles of work stand out as the responsibilities of
a faithful person:

Recognize That Work Is Essential.   Even before the fall,
God instituted work as a part of creation. "The Lord God
took the man and put him into the garden of Eden to
cultivate it and keep it" (Genesis 2:15, NASB). Despite
what many have come to think, work is not a result of the
curse!

In fact, work is so important that in Exodus 34:21 God
gives this command: "You shall work six days, but on the
seventh day you shall rest" (NASB).

Paul is just as direct when he says, "If anyone will not
work, neither let him eat" (2 Thessalonians 3:10, NASB).
This principle is an obvious contradiction to the practice of
our society today with its welfare and unemployment
programs. Examine the verse carefully. It says, "If anyone
will not work . . . ." It did not say, "If anyone *can* not
work. . . ." This principle does not apply to those who are
physically unable to work. This is for those who are able,
but choose not to work.

The wisdom of this is very real to our family. A close
friend has a sister in her mid-thirties who has always
been supported by her parents. She has never had to face
the responsibilities and the hardships involved in a job. As
a result, she is hopelessly immature in her financial life.

Work Hard, But Do Not Overwork.   Paul's life was a
model of hard work: "Now here is a command, dear

brothers, given in the name of our Lord Jesus Christ by
his authority: Stay away from any Christian who spends
his days in laziness and does not follow the ideal of hard
work we set up for you . . . follow our example."

Working hard must be balanced by the other priorities
of life. Clearly our first priority is Christ, "Seek first his
kingdom and his righteousness" (Matthew 6:33, NASB).
The second priority is the family.

If your job demands so much of your time and energy
that you neglect your relationship with Christ or your
family, then you are working too hard. You should then
determine whether the job is too demanding or your work
habits need changing. If you love to work, take extra
precautions to guard against forsaking the other priorities
of life.

*Recognize That All Honest Professions Are
Honorable.*   According to Scripture there is dignity in all
types of work: Adam was a farmer, Abraham a rancher,
Joseph an administrator, David a shepherd, Paul a
tentmaker, and Jesus a carpenter.

In their outstanding book, *Your Job, Survival or
Satisfaction?*, the Whites ask, "Are people really equal?
Yes, they are of equal worth in God's sight. But they are
not equal in ability or attainment. People have widely
varied abilities, manual skills, and intellectual capacities.
God has given each of us the ability to do certain things
well (Romans 12:6). We must recognize that some are
more intelligent or more skillful. It is not a matter of
'better or worse,' just different.

"Are laboring or unskilled jobs demeaning? The
answer is a resounding no! It is no biblically. It is no in
terms of value to society. It is no in regard to human
worth. It is no in the eyes of the law. It is yes only in the
warped value system of a materially corrupt society. A
person's value is not in what he does, but in who he is."[15]

In God's economy there is equal dignity in the labor of
the automobile mechanic and the president of General
Motors.

Develop Proper Employee-Employer Relationships.
Employees: In Colossians 3:23, 24, Paul says, "[Slaves]
work hard and cheerfully at all you do, just as though you
were working for the Lord and not merely for your
masters, remembering that it is the Lord Christ who is
going to pay you . . . . He is the one you are really working
for." Slaves are commanded to work hard and cheerfully
for their masters. In today's world this is the same as the
employee-employer relationship.

A good employee has several responsibilities:
obedience, faithful performance of assigned tasks, and the
willingness to work a full day for a full day's wage. Some
employees never consider time wasted on the job as
belonging to their employer. However, when they waste
the time of their employer, they are in essence stealing
from that person.

Many of us work under the supervision of people whom
we really do not like. If we are committed to becoming
faithful stewards, we need to see ourselves as "working for
the Lord." This is to be the attitude governing all man's
working responsibilities.

When Jim Seneff was in the Army he escaped
resentment and dissatisfaction by deciding to "work for
the Lord." Because he served obediently and faithfully, no
matter who was giving the orders, he remained content
during his entire Army experience.

Employers: "You slave owners [employers] must be just
and fair to all your slaves [employees]. Always remember
that you, too, have a Master in heaven" (Colossians 4:1).
The employer has an even greater responsibility to his
employees. He should be sensitive to their needs, consider
fairly their requests, and pay them a fair wage promptly
(Leviticus 19:13).

Too often employers have concentrated solely on
producing a profit at the expense of their personnel.
However, the Bible directs the employer to balance his
efforts to make a profit with an unselfish concern for his
employees.

Pursue Excellence. "Whatever you do, do your work heartily, as for the Lord rather than for men" (Colossians 3:23, NASB). Our work should be at such a level so that people will never equate mediocrity with God. Nothing less than the pursuit of excellence pleases the Lord. We are not required to be "superworkers" . . . persons of unlimited talents who never make mistakes. Rather, the Lord expects us to do the best we possibly can.

Governor Mark Hatfield said it this way: "Our first responsibility is to utilize and mobilize the resources, the capacity, the intellect, the drive, the ambitions and all that God has given us, and to use them to the fullest . . . your first responsibility is to perform with the highest degree of excellence."[16]

We must limit our pursuits to those we can handle with excellence. The extent and type of our activities should depend upon our individual capacity and ability.

An accountant in our town is known as a nice guy—in fact *too* nice. When anyone asks him to work on a project, he invariably accepts. His desk is littered with unfinished work. Nothing is completed on schedule. He has the reputation of a mediocre accountant simply because he is involved in far too many projects to do any well.

I, too, have a similar tendency to have "too many balls in the air." Frankly, I do not have the capacity to do an excellent job when my efforts are fragmented. I am learning to concentrate on one activity at a time. My office is not as "busy" as it used to be, but the quality of work has markedly improved.

Someone has said, "Work as unto the Lord . . . the pay's not always great, but the retirement benefits are out of this world!" And I would add one more benefit—increased satisfaction of a job done to the best of our ability.

Let everyone be sure that he is doing his very best, for then he will have the personal satisfaction of work well done.
                                                          Galatians 6:4

GOD'S PART IN WORK

In Chapter 3 (God's Part) we learned that God is in control of all events, including the circumstances surrounding our work. He also makes clear his specific responsibilities in connection with our work:

1) God gives us our ability. "God has given each of us the ability to do certain things well" (Romans 12:6).

2) God gives each man his measure of intelligence. "He gives wise men their wisdom, and scholars their intelligence" (Daniel 2:21).

3) God gives us wealth. "It is the Lord your God who gives you power to become rich" (Deuteronomy 8:18).

4) God controls our promotions. "For promotion and power come from nowhere on earth, but only from God" (Psalm 75:6).

Once we have done our part in work to the best of our ability, then we can be satisfied knowing it is God's decision whether to prosper and promote us. Still, as with Joseph in the house of Potiphar, there may be be times when I do not prosper even though I have been faithful in my work. Other times God may choose to prosper me in my work as the Lord did later with Joseph as prime minister of Egypt.

CONTRAST

Society says: Either work as little as possible because labor is distasteful; or work as much as possible because your job is all-important.

Scripture says: Work as unto the Lord with excellence as your standard. Work hard, but do not overwork.

COMMITMENT

Prayerfully evaluate your attitudes toward work and your job performance in light of what Scripture teaches. To help you discover any areas that need changing, ask yourself these questions:

1) Would I work more conscientiously if Jesus were my boss?

2) Would I think more highly of a president of an oil company than a gas station attendant?

3) How is my relationship with my employer, employees, and fellow-workers?

4) Am I trying to do too much?

5) Am I performing my job at the level of excellence?

6) Am I lazy? Do I work hard?

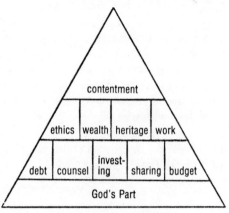

THE PYRAMID OF CONTENTMENT

FIFTEEN
CONTENTMENT—A SECRET
LEARNED, NOT EARNED

*Let your way of life be free from the love of money, being
content with what you have; for He Himself said, "I will
never desert you, nor will I ever forsake you."*

Hebrews 13:5, NASB

I was invited to attend the second anniversary of a very
special event. May 1, 1976 was the day the Hitchcocks
reached their goal of becoming debt-free. Two years later
they were just as grateful for their new freedom and, more
importantly, their marriage was growing stronger.

It had been a rugged struggle for them. Several times
they had been on the verge of quitting, but the stakes of
saving their marriage were too high. They persevered,
reached their goal, and were now enjoying a marriage
with greater contentment than they had ever before
experienced.

Allen and Jean had discovered what millions of people
have learned through history: the Bible is a blueprint for
living.

The result of your reading and following these
principles is that you will learn the secret of contentment.

I know how to live on almost nothing or with everything. I have learned the secret of contentment in every situation, whether it be a full stomach or hunger, plenty or want; for I can do everything God asks me to do with the help of Christ.
Philippians 4:12, 13

What is the secret of contentment? To know what God requires of a good and faithful steward, doing those requirements, and by faith trusting that the Lord will do God's part. Note that Paul says that when we do everything God asks, there will be contentment. It is not just knowing these things that brings contentment; it is doing them.

As Francis Schaeffer said, "These two words, *know* and *do*, occur throughout Scripture and always in that order. We cannot do until we know, but we can know without doing. The house built on the rock is the house of the man who knows and does. The house built on the sand is the house of the man who knows but does not do." [17]

I would like to emphasize the importance of knowing and doing in learning the secret of contentment. Remember Daniel, the faithful steward:

They could find no ground of accusation or evidence of corruption, inasmuch as he [Daniel] was faithful, and no negligence or corruption was to be found in him.
Daniel 6:4, NASB

Daniel knew the principles of faithfulness and he did them (no negligence or corruption), so he was a contented man with a clear conscience before his God and king—even when faced with the extreme circumstances of a lions' den.

I do not know your circumstances. They may be financially extreme, seemingly hopeless. But if you grasp God's part and your part and act in faith, you can be content with the assurance that God is in absolute control of your situation. God may choose to deliver you from your "lion" as he did with Daniel, or you may continue to suffer as did many in the Roman coliseums.

Daniel was content, not because he was certain God would save him from the lions, but because he knew that whatever happened was the sovereign decision of his loving and merciful God. In Romans 8:28 we learn that, "God causes all things to work together for good to those who love God, to those who are called according to his purpose" (NASB).

During times of difficulty, it is not easy to recognize that good will result, but in the next verse we discover why we can have confidence in any situation: "For whom He foreknew, He also predestined to become conformed to the image of His Son" Romans 8:29, (NASB). Every situation, even the severe one, is designed to prepare us to become more intimately related to Jesus.

While I was integrating the principles of being a faithful steward into my life, my business suddenly ground to a screeching halt.

At that time I was involved in selling properties that had been in our family for years. I was as hard-working and conscientious as I had ever been in my life . . . and for a year sold absolutely nothing. I even tried to sell our mint-condition Volkswagen at a bargain price, and the purchaser returned it!

It was during this frustrating time that God taught me an important lesson. Although I knew God's principles of being a faithful steward and had applied them, I had not placed my faith in the living Lord to do God's part. I knew what part God was to play, but I had put my faith in the principles, which are good, but they are not to be the objects of faith. Our faith is to be in the sufficiency and faithfulness of Jesus Christ.

The next year when the property finally began to sell, I was astonished at my emotional detachment. I was grateful, but I had lost some of the excitement that business had previously given me.

I had experienced how God could give wealth or take it away whenever he wanted. I was simply called to be a faithful steward of his assets. I was learning to be content.

In *Living on Less and Liking It More* Maxine Hancock describes contentment as, "Similar to happiness, that greatly sought-after but always elusive goal of society. However, it is deeper and more fulfilling than happiness. It is a quiet plateau that can be reached internally even when there seems little external reason for it.

"I am not pretending that the learning process is always fun or easy. But the Spirit of God is a thorough and loving teacher and, of all the joys of life, it is contentment . . . for which I am most grateful."[18]

A good friend once asked me what was the most valuable lesson I had learned from our seminars. I've had time to reflect on that question some time now, and I think the most valuable lesson has been the realization that I needed to consistently review Scripture. I noticed this in preparation for the seminar. If I had invested little time studying Scripture during the previous weeks, I would discover that I had been molded ever-so-subtly by the views of our society.

In Romans 12:2 Paul presented this problem and the solution: "And do not be conformed to this world, but be transformed by the renewing of your mind" (NASB). The only way for any of us to renew our minds (to preserve the correct perspective) is to continually expose ourselves to Scripture.

The Bible has the answers to the financial problems of the sophisticated twentieth century. The eternal principles of Scripture are practical in any culture and in any century.

THE FINANCIAL BEATITUDES

1) Blessed is the man who is out of debt, for he shall be free.

2) Blessed is the man who seeks godly counsel, for he shall receive wisdom.

3) Blessed is the man who works as unto the Lord, for he shall stand before kings.

4) Blessed is the man of integrity, for he shall have a clear conscience.

5) Blessed is the man who saves, for he shall be able to provide for his family.

6) Blessed is the man who shares mercifully, for he shall receive mercy.

7) Blessed is the man who budgets, for he shall have enough at the end of the month.

8) Blessed is the man who is a good and faithful steward, for he shall be content in every circumstance.

QUESTIONS & ANSWERS

This section deals with some frequently asked and sometimes
controversial questions. When Scripture does not specifically answer the
question, my opinion is given to stimulate your thinking.

Question: Is a Depression coming soon? If so, how should a person
prepare to survive?

Answer: I am not an economic forecaster and do not know what the
economy will be like in five years. However, America and most of the
nations of the world are violating scriptural principles of handling
money—particularly in the area of debt. And I believe that you cannot
continue to violate a scriptural principle without suffering the
consequences. I do not know if it will happen next week or twenty years
from now, but if we do not stop violating scripture, we will definitely pay
the price.

The only way for us to prepare for economic chaos is by being faithful
stewards: Eliminate all debt, become excellent in our work, establish a
program of saving and investing, share liberally, and then trust God
for his provision—even in a Depression.

I am convinced that if we should go through an economic depression,
the faithful, contented steward will stand out from the crowd that has
built its happiness on favorable circumstances. It should be a fantastic
opportunity to share the hope that is within us.

Question: What is the Christian perspective on paying taxes?

Answer: This is an excellent example of the contrast between society
and Scripture. Avoid paying taxes at any cost, our culture says; after all,
the government wastes money at every turn—fat cats in Washington,
welfare fraud, the bureaucrats, etc.

Entire financial industries are built around the practice of avoiding taxes. I have seen many investments that were sold, not because they made sound economic sense, but because they were advertised as "tax shelters."

There is a very fine line between tax avoidance and tax evasion, and there is a strong temptation to misappropriate funds that are legally due our government. An estimated $50 billion a year in taxes is lost in tax evasion.

I am not condoning the waste and excesses found in government. In fact, I believe a citizen should make an effort to influence government to be more efficient and responsive. But the Bible tells us of an additional responsibility: pay your taxes gladly!

Obey the laws, then, for two reasons: first, to keep from being punished, and second, just because you know you should. Pay your taxes too, for these same two reasons. For government workers need to be paid so that they can keep doing God's work, serving you. Pay everyone whatever he ought to have: pay your taxes and import duties gladly.

Romans 13:5–7

We have so much to be thankful for in America. The government provides many services we take for granted—highways, fire protection, potable water, etc. So pay your taxes gladly—this has revolutionized my attitude and I have a renewed sense of contentment around tax time when many are quite discontent.

Question: Should I borrow to buy an automobile?

Answer: If possible, pay cash for your car. However, most people simply do not have the cash to acquire a car without borrowing. The car is a major purchase and approximately two out of three borrow to buy their car.

If you must borrow, I have three suggestions:

1) Shop for the best deal in financing your car. In general, the most expensive sources of automobile credit are the car dealers and finance companies. Credit unions and commercial banks are usually the least expensive.

2) Pray that God would provide a good, inexpensive used car to minimize your borrowing, or better yet to allow you to pay cash.

Last year it was necessary for Bev and me to get a second vehicle. We listed our requirements: a small pickup truck, in good mechanical condition, at a price of less than $500. We then prayed.

After three months a neighbor learned of our search. He owned a low-mileage Datsun pickup in reasonable condition. He needed the truck once a month, but could no longer afford the insurance.

We bought the truck with the understanding that he could drive it the one day a month it was needed. The cost—$100! I firmly believe that we can experience the reality of God by praying about our spending decisions, and waiting to see his active involvement in meeting our needs.

3) Begin saving the money to buy your next car.

By purchasing the low-cost used truck, we have been able to save the amount that would have been going toward car payments. Each month we put the "car payment" in a separate savings account to accumulate enough cash to pay for our next car.

This is only one of many methods you can use to save. The key you can use to break the car financing habit is to *begin saving now for your next car.*

Question: Should wives work?

Answer: That question is a paradox. All wives work—whether they are homemakers or work outside the home. A Stanford University study shows that wives who work outside the home carry a particularly heavy load of seventy to eighty hours a week with the responsibilities of their job *plus* homework.

The trend for wives to hold jobs is escalating rapidly. In 1947, working husbands outnumbered working wives five to one; now the ratio is less than two to one. For many reasons, women are becoming involved in jobs of all kinds. Wives work to provide additional income for their families and to express their creativity; and widows and divorcees work to provide for the needs of their families.

When young children are at home in their formative years, it is wise for a mother to remain at home, working only in extreme circumstances.

These older women must train the younger women to live quietly, to love their husbands and their children, and to be sensible and clean minded, spending their time in their own homes . . . .

Titus 2:4

Proverbs 31 paints a beautiful picture of the working wife living a balanced life with the thrust of her activity toward the home. My opinion is that woman's work is not so much *in* the home as it is *for* the home. Proverbs 31 does not say that a wife should be confined to four walls, but involved in activities that relate to the home. I believe there are three broad justifications for a wife working outside the home:

1) When her salary helps to provide for family needs. Many times when the husband is in college, the wife works to provide the family's needs.

2) When professional talents or spiritual gifts are evident and no children are at home.

3) When the creativity and resourcefulness of a wife's hobbies and talents allow the family to be involved and not forsaken.

Question: Should a Christian declare bankruptcy?

Answer: In the 1970's five of the ten largest bankruptcies in the history of American business occurred, capped by the collapse of the W. T. Grant retail chain. Bankruptcy knocks on the doors of individuals who earn as little as $100 a week, as well as multi-million dollar corporations. Indeed, there are nine times as many personal bankruptcies as there are corporate bankruptcies. In fact, personal bankruptcies now approach 250,000 a year.

Although the stigma of bankruptcy has rapidly diminished in recent years, I believe Scripture teaches that bankruptcy is not the normal way of getting out of debt.

Evil men borrow and "cannot pay it back !" But the good man returns what he owes with some extra besides.

Psalm 37:21

The Bible teaches that you should repay your debts. This has to be balanced. If you were an owner (a stockholder) of W. T. Grant, you might have some difficulty in paying Grant's $1 billion of indebtedness.

As a rule of thumb for determining your responsibilities for debt repayment: If you were intimately involved in the accumulation of the debts, you should intend to pay them back; if you were not actively involved, such as a stockholder in W. T. Grant, you probably are not responsible for their repayment.

Once responsibility is determined, make every effort to establish a schedule of repayment with your creditors and then adhere to the schedule.

I know of couples who have been forced into bankruptcy by unreasonable creditors. But once again, the only responsibility of a faithful steward is to do our part. And our part is to diligently try to pay back debts, to try to avoid bankruptcy, and to recognize that God's part is to control the circumstances surrounding a potential bankruptcy.

Question: Should Christians expect to prosper?

Answer: John Wesley is quoted as saying, "True religion 'a personal relationship with Jesus Christ) will result in the people of a nation becoming more hard-working, honest, frugal, and thrifty, which results in the creation of wealth."

I think Wesley is correct. Christians who follow the principles of a faithful steward should expect to prosper. However, there are four reasons they may not:

Character: God wants to develop our character. Joseph is an illustration of how God developed character in a man's life by taking away his prosperity. Although he had been faithful, Joseph went through some difficult situations, losing all he had as God built his character to prepare him to eventually be elevated to number-two man in the kingdom of Egypt.

We also exult in our tribulations; knowing that tribulation brings about perseverance; and perseverance, proven character.

Romans 5:3, 4, NASB

Discipline: In the Old Testament there were a number of times when God took away the wealth of the nation of Israel to discipline them and bring them back to himself. Similarly, in the New Testament John told his friend Gaius, "I pray that in all respects you may prosper . . . just as your soul prospers" (3 John 2, NASB).

I believe that God will lovingly withhold prosperity if it will bring us closer to him. It has been interesting the last several years to watch how a number of people in our community have changed their values as a result of the recession we had in the mid-1970's. As they lost their wealth, it gave them the motivation to question what really is important in life and turn to the Lord.

Nothing is certain in life: Bill Stephens, a local residential real estate broker and a good friend of mine, is a hard-working professional who has made excellence his goal. I asked him what was the most important issue God had taught him through his work. He replied with respect in his voice, "Nothing in this life is certain except the Lord and his Word."

Enjoy prosperity whenever you can, and when hard times strike, realize that God gives one as well as the other—so that everyone will realize that nothing is certain in this life.

Ecclesiastes 7:14

He then explained that the purchase of a home is usually the major purchase a person will make, and often emotions run high.

"I am compensated only if the sale is consummated," he said, "and I have learned the hard way that there is no such thing as a sure sale. But it is precisely this constant uncertainty in my business, coupled with the realization that God controls the circumstances, that has made me a more relaxed and contented person in all areas of life."

God may choose not to prosper us: Daniel and Jeremiah were two prophets who lived during the period of the Babylonian captivity. Each had a dramatically different economic status.

Daniel was prime minister of the Babylonian Empire. He must have lived in a fine home staffed with servants, earned a handsome salary, and had the finest "Cadillac chariot" . . . and Daniel was a faithful man.

Jeremiah was poor. He was repeatedly imprisoned, ridiculed, and impoverished. Yet, he also was a faithful man.

These faithful men were each at a different end of the economic spectrum. God in his infinite wisdom and mercy sovereignly chooses which of his faithful people he will prosper.

Question: Should a Christian carry insurance?

Answer: The basic purpose of insurance is to spread the risk of loss. Let's examine three types of insurance.

1) Self-insurance—a refusal to pay premiums to an insurance company to spread the risk of loss from sickness, casualty or loss of life. The person hopes to meet contingencies out of personal reserves or subsequent provision.

2) Purchased insurance—payment of premiums to an insurance company to spread various risks of loss.

132 Your Money: Frustration or Freedom?

3) Faith insurance—to trust in other Christians or divine intervention, to make provision in the event of loss.

Frequently state laws or contracts provide for insurance requirements. We are to be subject to governmental authorities and keep our contractual promises. Responsibilities to creditors and family frequently demand that we carry insurance.

To purchase insurance does not mean we have a lack of faith.

The concept of "100 percent ownership by God" might lead one to self-insurance, but the concept of "100 percent stewardship" probably leads toward purchased insurance.

Question: What does Scripture say should be my standard of living?

Answer: There is much talk about life-style today. There are hundreds of books on how to become rich, and an entire subculture has developed to try to break the "tyranny of things" and return to the "simple, natural" way of living.

Nobody lacks information regarding the outward details of practically any standard of living. However, when we look for specific guidelines on how much and what we should possess, Scripture is pointedly silent. The reason is that biblical life-style is not primarily concerned with our external possessions.

However, I believe that as we come to know Jesus and his Word more intimately, there will inevitably be a distinction between how we choose to spend our money and how those who are oriented to totally different values spend their money.

The key to the life-style of a faithful steward lies primarily in the proper inner attitude toward his possessions. Scripture calls us to an inner reality in our relationship with Jesus Christ rather than to prescribed appearances and amounts of possessions. The decision as to how much one should have is between a man and his God.

SCRIPTURES

GOD'S PART

I. OWNERSHIP

A. God Is the Creator

Psalm 146:6 . . . . God who made both earth and heaven, the seas and everything in them. He is the God who keeps every promise.

Isaiah 44:24. The Lord, your Redeemer who made you, says, All things were made by me; I alone stretched out the heavens. By myself I made the earth and everything in it.

Colossians 1:15–17. Christ is the exact likeness of the unseen God. He existed before God made anything at all, and, in fact, Christ himself is the Creator who made everything in heaven and earth, the things we can see and the things we can't; the spirit world with its kings and kingdoms, its rulers and authorities; all were made by Christ for his own use and glory. He was before all else began and it is his power that holds everything together.

Revelation 4:11. O Lord, you are worthy to receive the glory and honor and the power, for you created all things. They were created and called into being by your act of will.

Genesis 1:1–27; Exodus 4:11, 12; 2 Kings 19:15; 1 Chronicles 16:26; Nehemiah 9:6; Job 26:7–14; Psalm 19:1; 33:6–9; 89:11, 12; 94:8, 9; 95:5; 96:5; 102:25; 104:1–26; 119:90, 91; 121:2; 146:6; 148:1–6; 150:1; Proverbs 8:29; 22:2; Isaiah 37:16; 44:24; 45:18; 48:12, 13; Acts 7:48–50; 14:15; 1 Corinthians 8:6; Colossians 1:15–17; Hebrews 3:4; Revelation 4:11; 10:6; 14:7.

B. God Is the Owner

Leviticus 25:23. And remember, the land is mine, so you may not sell it permanently. You are merely my tenants and sharecroppers!

1 Chronicles 29:11, 14. Yours is the mighty power and glory and victory and majesty. Everything in the heavens and earth is yours, O Lord, and this is your kingdom. But who am I and who are my people that we should be permitted to give anything to you? Everything we have has come from you, and we only give you what is yours already!

Psalm 50:10–12. For all the animals of field and forest are mine! The cattle on a thousand hills! And all the birds upon the mountains! If I were hungry, I would not mention it to you—for all the world is mine and everything in it.

Haggai 2:8 (KJV). The silver is mine, and the gold is mine, saith the Lord of hosts.

1 Corinthians 10:26. For the earth and every good thing in it belongs to the Lord and is yours to enjoy.

Exodus 19:5; Leviticus 25:23; Deuteronomy 10:14; 1 Chronicles 29:11, 14; Job 41:11; Psalm 24:1, 2; 50:10–12; 82:8; 95:3–5; Haggai 2:8; 1 Corinthians 6:20; 7:23; 10:26; 2 Corinthians 1:22.

II. SITUATIONS

A. God Is in Control of Circumstances

1 Samuel 2:6–8. The Lord kills, the Lord gives life. Some he causes to be poor and others to be rich. He cuts one down and lifts another up. He lifts the poor from the dust—Yes, from a pile of ashes—and treats them as princes sitting in the seats of honor. For all the earth is the Lord's and he has set the world in order.

1 Chronicles 29:11, 12. Yours is the mighty power and glory and victory and majesty. Everything in the heavens and earth is yours, O Lord, and this is your kingdom. We adore you as being in control of everything. Riches and honor come from you alone, and you are the Ruler of all mankind; your hand controls power and might, and it is at your discretion that men are made great and given strength.

Psalm 29:10, 11. At the Flood, the Lord showed his control of all creation. Now he continues to unveil his power. He will give his people strength. He will bless them with peace.

Psalm 139:1–5, 13–16. O Lord, you have examined my heart and know everything about me. You know when I sit or stand. When far away you know my every thought. You chart the path ahead of me, and tell me where to stop and rest. Every moment, you know where I am. You know what I am going to say before I even say it. You both precede and follow me, and place your hand of blessing on my head. You made all the delicate, inner parts of my body, and knit them together in my mother's

womb. Thank you for making me so wonderfully complex! It is amazing
to think about. Your workmanship is marvelous—and how well I know
it. You were there while I was being formed in utter seclusion! You saw
me before I was born and scheduled each day of my life before I began to
breathe. Every day was recorded in your Book!

Ecclesiastes 7:14. Enjoy prosperity whenever you can, and when hard
times strike, realize that God gives one as well as the other—so that
everyone will realize that nothing is certain in this life.

Jeremiah 5:22. I [the Lord] set the shorelines of the world by perpetual
decrees, so that the oceans, though they toss and roar, can never pass
those bounds. Isn't such a God to be feared and worshiped?

Genesis 45:4, 5, 8; 50:20; Deuteronomy 10:17, 18; Joshua 14:1, 2; Judges
7:7, 22; 1 Samuel 2:6–8; 18:14; 2 Samuel 12:7, 8; 1 Chronicles 16:31; 18:6;
22:9; 23:25; 29:11, 12; 2 Chronicles 15:15; 16:9; 20:6, 15; Ezra 7:9;
Nehemiah 4:15; 6:15, 16; Job 9:1–11; 12:17–25; 28:23–28; 37:6, 7, 10–13;
38:1–41; 39:1–30; Psalm 29:10, 11; 65:9, 10; 74:12–17; 81:10; 83:17, 18;
89:9; 91:1–7; 93:2; 107:23–28, 33–42; 135:5, 6; 139:1–5, 13–16; 147:5, 8,
9, 12–14; Proverbs 16:1, 33; 29:13; Ecclesiastes 7:14; Isaiah 1:26; 14:26,
27; 19:11–14; 40:12, 13, 21–29; 41:4; 42:5; 45:4–8, 12, 13; 46:9, 10; 48:15;
Jeremiah 5:22; 10:12, 13; 31:35; 32:27, 37–42; 33:6, 7; 43:9–11; Ezekiel
11:5; 36:28–30, 36; 39:28; Daniel 2:20–23; 4:34, 35, 37; Amos 4:6–13;
Acts 7:10; 14:16, 17; Ephesians 1:4, 11; Hebrews 1:3.

B. God Controls Promotions and Success

Psalm 75:6, 7. For promotion and power come from nowhere on earth,
but only from God. He promotes one and deposes another.

Daniel 4:17. The purpose of this decree is that all the world may
understand that the Most High dominates the kingdoms of the world,
and gives them to anyone he wants to, even the lowliest of men!

Zechariah 4:6. This is God's message to Zerubbabel: "Not by might, nor
by power, but by my Spirit, says the Lord of Hosts—you will succeed
because of my Spirit, though you are few and weak."

2 Samuel 7:8, 9; 23:1; 1 Kings 2:24; 10:9; 16:2; 2 Kings 9:6; 1 Chronicles
11:9; 17:7–10; 28:4; 2 Chronicles 1:1; 17:5; 26:15; Psalm 21:3–5; 30:6, 7;
62:7; 71:6, 7; 75:6, 7; Isaiah 22:15–20; Jeremiah 1:10; Daniel 2:37, 38;
4:17, 25; Zechariah 4:6; Luke 1:51–53.

C. God Controls Prosperity, Abundance, and Blessings

Genesis 24:34, 35. "I am Abraham's servant," he explained. "And
Jehovah has overwhelmed my master with blessings so that he is a great
man among the people of his land. God has given him flocks of sheep and
herds of cattle, and a fortune in silver and gold, and many slaves and
camels and donkeys."

Deuteronomy 8:18. Always remember that it is the Lord your God who
gives you power to become rich . . . .

1 Corinthians 4:7. What are you so puffed up about? What do you have that God hasn't given you? And if all you have is from God, why act as though you are so great, and as though you have accomplished something on your own?

Genesis 12:1–3; 14:19, 20; 15:1; 21:22; 24:1, 34, 35; 25:11; 26:12, 28; Leviticus 26:10; Deuteronomy 8:18; 28:2–8, 11, 12; 30:9; 2 Kings 18:5–7; 2 Chronicles 1:12; 25:9; 26:5; Ezra 1:2; 7:6; Job 5:8–11; 42:12; Psalm 66:12; 85:12; 106:4, 5; 115:12, 13; Jeremiah 33:11; Ezekiel 16:9–14; Hosea 2:8, 9; Zephaniah 2:7; 3:20; Haggai 2:18, 19; Zechariah 1:16, 17; 3:10; 8:12; Romans 10:12; 1 Corinthians 4:7.

D. God Controls the Thoughts and Emotions

Exodus 12:36. And the Lord gave the Israelis favor with the Egyptians, so that they gave them whatever they wanted. And the Egyptians were practically stripped of everything they owned!

Exodus 11:3; 12:36; 1 Samuel 10:26; 1 Kings 8:58; 1 Chronicles 14:17; 2 Chronicles 36:22, 23; Ezra 1:5; 7:27; 9:9; Daniel 1:9.

E. God Controls the Giving of Special Abilities

Romans 12:6. God has given each of us the ability to do certain things well.

Ephesians 4:7, 8. Christ has given each of us special abilities—whatever he wants us to have out of his rich storehouse of gifts. The Psalmist tells us about this, for he says that when Christ returned triumphantly to heaven after his resurrection and victory over Satan, he gave generous gifts to men.

Exodus 31:1–3, 6; 35:34, 35; 36:1, 2; 1 Kings 3:12, 28; 4:29; 5:12; 18:46; 2 Chronicles 9:23; Daniel 1:17; Romans 12:6, 8; 1 Corinthians 12:1; Ephesians 4:7; 1 Timothy 4:14, 15.

III. PROVISION

A. God Promises to Provide Food and Needs

Psalm 33:18, 19. But the eyes of the Lord are watching over those who fear him, who rely upon his steady love. He will keep them from death even in times of famine!

Psalm 37:25, 26. I have been young and now I am old. And in all my years I have never seen the Lord forsake a man who loves him; nor have I seen the children of the godly go hungry. Instead, the godly are able to be generous with their gifts and loans to others, and their children are a blessing.

Matthew 6:31–33. So don't worry at all about having enough food and clothing. Why be like the heathen? For they take pride in all these things and are deeply concerned about them. But your heavenly Father already knows perfectly well that you need them, and he will give them to you if you give him first place in your life and live as he wants you to.

Luke 12:30, 31. All mankind scratches for its daily bread, but your heavenly Father knows your needs. He will always give you all you need from day to day if you will make the Kingdom of God your primary concern.

Genesis 1:29, 30; Exodus 16:17, 18; 23:25, 26; Leviticus 26:3–6; Deuteronomy 8:2–5, 11–17; Ruth 1:6, 7; 1 Kings 17:14–16; Ezra 8:23; Nehemiah 9:21; Job 10:11, 12; Psalm 16:5; 23:1–3; 33:18–20; 34:9, 10; 37:17–19, 25, 26; 68:9; 78:15, 19–29; 81:16; 104:27, 28; 111:4–6; 136:25; 145:15, 16; Proverbs 10:3; Isaiah 26:7; Jeremiah 31:14; Matthew 6:11, 25–33; 14:17–22; 15:34–38; 16:8–11; Mark 6:35–44; 8:5–9, 19–21; Luke 9:13–17; 12:22–31; John 6:7–13; Acts 17:25, 26; Romans 11:32–36; Revelation 7:15–17.

B. God Provides for the Poor

Psalm 12:5. The Lord replies, "I will arise and defend the oppressed, the poor, the needy. I will rescue them as they have longed for me to do." The Lord's promise is sure.

Psalm 10:14; 12:5; 69:33; 72:2–5, 12, 13; 82:3, 4; 102:17; 109:31; 113:5–9; 140:11, 12; Proverbs 15:25; Isaiah 25:1–4; Jeremiah 22:3, 4.

OUR PART

I. FAITHFUL STEWARDSHIP

A. Our Authority to Be Stewards

Psalm 8:6. You have put him in charge of everything you made; everything is put under his authority.

Genesis 1:28; 9:2, 3; Psalm 8:6, 7; 115:16; Galatians 4:7.

B. Our Responsibility to Be Stewards

1 Cor. 4:2. Now the most important thing about a servant is that he does just what his master tells him to.

Deuteronomy 5:32, 33; 8:11; Ezra 9:12; Job 36:11, 12; Psalm 119:36; 128:1, 2; Proverbs 22:4; Isaiah 1:19; Jeremiah 7:21–23; Matthew 4:4; 1 Cor. 4:2.

C. Examples of Faithful Stewards

Daniel 6:4, 22. This made the other presidents and governors very jealous, and they began searching for some fault in the way Daniel was handling his affairs so they could complain to the king about him. But they couldn't find anything to criticize! He was faithful and honest, and made no mistakes . . . . "My God has sent his angel," he said, "to shut the lions' mouths so that they can't touch me; for I am innocent before God, nor, sir, have I wronged you."

Acts 20:33–35. "I have never been hungry for money or fine clothing—you know that these hands of mine worked to pay my own way and even to supply the needs of those who were with me. And I was a constant example to you in helping the poor; for I remembered the words of the Lord Jesus, 'It is more blessed to give than to receive.' "

Genesis 31:38–42; 1 Kings 3:6; 2 Kings 12:15; 22:7; 1 Chronicles 9:22, 26–29; Nehemiah 5:14–16, 18, 19; 7:2; Daniel 6:4, 21; Matthew 25:14–29; Luke 19:12–26; Acts 20:33–35; Hebrews 6:10.

D. Faithfulness and Results of Faithfulness

Luke 16:10–12. For unless you are honest in small matters, you won't be in large ones. If you cheat even a little, you won't be honest with greater responsibilities. And if you are untrustworthy about worldly wealth, who will trust you with the true riches of heaven? And if you are not faithful with other people's money, why should you be entrusted with money of your own?

Matthew 6:24; 13:13; Luke 8:18; 12:42–44; 16:10–14; 2 Timothy 2:15.

E. Unfaithfulness

Ezekiel 16:17; Luke 16:1–9.

DEBT

I. SCRIPTURAL PERSPECTIVE OF DEBT

Deuteronomy 28:1, 2, 12. If you fully obey all of these commandments of the Lord your God, the laws I am declaring to you today, God will transform you into the greatest nation in the world. These are the blessings that will come upon you . . . you shall lend to many nations, but you shall not borrow from them.

Deuteronomy 28:15, 16, 43, 44. If you won't listen to the Lord your God and won't obey these laws I am giving you today, then all of these curses shall come upon you . . . . Foreigners living among you shall become richer and richer while you become poorer and poorer. They shall lend to you, not you to them! They shall be the head and you shall be the tail!

Proverbs 22:7. Just as the rich rule the poor, so the borrower is servant to the lender.

Romans 13:8. Pay all your debts except the debt of love for others—never finish paying that!

II. EXAMPLES OF THE HARDSHIP OF DEBT

2 Kings 4:1; Matthew 5:25, 26; 18:23–34.

III. IF YOU ARE IN DEBT, WHEN SHOULD YOU BEGIN TO GET OUT?

Proverbs 3:27, 28. Don't withhold repayment of your debts. Don't say "some other time," if you can pay now.

Proverbs 3:27, 28; Matthew 5:25, 26.

IV. HOW MUCH OF OUR DEBT SHOULD WE PAY?

Psalm 37:21. Evil men borrow and "cannot pay it back"! But the good man returns what he owes with some extra besides.

Psalm 37:21; Romans 13:8.

V. OLD TESTAMENT DEBT REDUCTION

Leviticus 25:8–10, 24–27, 29–31, 39–41; Deuteronomy 15: 1, 2.

COSIGNING

I. IT IS POOR JUDGMENT TO COSIGN

Proverbs 17:18. It is poor judgment to countersign another's note, to become responsible for his debts.

Proverbs 22:26, 27. Unless you have the extra cash on hand, don't countersign a note. Why risk everything you own? They'll even take your bed!

Proverbs 1:13–15; 17:18; 22:26, 27; 27:13.

II. IF YOU HAVE COSIGNED, IMMEDIATELY REMOVE YOURSELF FROM LIABILITY

Proverbs 6:1–5. Son, if you endorse a note for someone you hardly know, guaranteeing his debt, you are in serious trouble. You may have trapped yourself by your agreement. Quick! Get out of it if you possibly can! Swallow your pride; don't let embarrassment stand in the way. Go and beg to have your name erased. Don't put it off. Do it now. Don't rest until you do. If you can get out of this trap you have saved yourself like a deer from a hunter, or a bird from the net.

COUNSEL

I. SEEK COUNSEL

A. We Are Admonished to Seek Counsel

Proverbs 19:20. Get all the advice you can and be wise the rest of your life.

Proverbs 12:15. A fool thinks he needs no advice, but a wise man listens to others.

Proverbs 10:8; 13:10; 19:20; 20:5, 18; 21:11; Luke 14:31.

B. Examples of Seeking Counsel

Esther 1:13-15. The king was furious, but first consulted his lawyers, for he did nothing without their advice. They were men of wisdom who knew the temper of the times as well as Persian law and justice.

Judges 20:7; 1 Kings 12:6-13; 1 Chronicles 13:1; 2 Chronicles 10:5-16; 20:21; Esther 1:13-15.

C. Results of Seeking Counsel

Ecclesiastes 4:9-12. Two can accomplish more than twice as much as one, for the results can be much better. If one falls, the other pulls him up; but if a man falls when he is alone, he's in trouble. Also, on a cold night, two under a blanket gain warmth from each other, but how can one be warm alone? And one standing alone can be attacked and defeated, but two can stand back-to-back and conquer; three is even better, for a triple-braided cord is not easily broken.

Proverbs 9:11; 11:14; 15:23; Ecclesiastes 4:9-12.

D. Results of Not Seeking Counsel

Proverbs 12:26. The good man asks advice from friends; the wicked plunge ahead—and fall.

2 Chronicles 25:16; 36:12; Proverbs 10:8; 12:26; Ecclesiastes 4:13.

E. Examples of Wise Counsel

Daniel 1:18-20. King Nebuchadnezzar had long talks with each of them, and none of them impressed him as much as Daniel, Hananiah, Misha-el, and Azariah. So they were put on his regular staff of advisors. And in all matters requiring information and balanced judgment, the king found these young men's advice ten times better than that of all the skilled magicians and wise astrologers in his realm.

Exodus 18:13-24; 1 Chronicles 27:32, 33; Esther 1:21; Job 29:21-25; Proverbs 10:20; 18:20; Daniel 1:19-21; 1 Corinthians 4:14; 12:8.

II. WHO SHOULD WE SEEK COUNSEL FROM?

A. From the Lord

Psalm 16:7. I will bless the Lord who counsels me; he gives me wisdom in the night. He tells me what to do.

Psalm 16:7; 32:8; 73:24; Proverbs 8:33; Isaiah 9:6; 30:1, 2; 31:1.

B. From Scripture

Psalm 119:24. Your laws are both my light and my counselors.

Psalm 19:7–11; 119:24, 96–100; Proverbs 2:6; 13:13.

C. From People

   1) *from godly people*
Psalm 37:30, 31. The godly man is a good counselor because he is just
and fair and knows right from wrong.

Psalm 16:3; 37:30, 31; Proverbs 10:21, 31; 13:20; 15:7.

   2) *from your father and mother*
Proverbs 6:20–23. Young man, obey your father and your mother. Tie
their instructions around your finger so you won't forget. Take to heart
all of their advice. Every day and all night long their counsel will lead
you and save you from harm; when you wake up in the morning, let
their instruction guide you into the new day. For their advice is a beam
of light directed into the dark corners of your mind to warn you of
danger and to give you a good life.

Proverbs 1:8, 9; 6:20–23; 15:5; 23:22.

   3) *from the wise*
Proverbs 13:14. The advice of a wise man refreshes like water from a
mountain spring.

D. Many Counselors Are Good

Proverbs 15:22. Plans go wrong with too few counselors; many counselors
bring success.

Proverbs 15:22; 24:6; Luke 14:31.

III. AVOID THE COUNSEL OF EVIL MEN

Psalm 1:1. Oh, the joys of those who do not follow evil men's advice, who
do not hang around with sinners, scoffing at the things of God.

2 Chronicles 22:3–5; Psalm 1:1–3; Proverbs 14:7; 24:7.

WORK

I. WORK IS NECESSARY

Exodus 34:21. You shall work six days.

2 Thessalonians 3:6–10. Now here is a command, dear brothers, given in
the name of our Lord Jesus Christ by his authority: Stay away from any

Christian who spends his days in laziness and does not follow the ideal of
hard work we set up for you. For you well know that you ought to follow
our example: you never saw us loafing; we never accepted food from
anyone without buying it; we worked hard day and night for the money
we needed to live on, in order that we would not be a burden to any of
you. It wasn't that we didn't have the right to ask you to feed us, but we
wanted to show you, firsthand, how you should work for your living.
Even while we were still there with you we gave you this rule: "He who
does not work shall not eat."

Genesis 2:15; 3:17 19; 1 Chronicles 22:16; 28:20; Proverbs 14:4; 16:26,
27; John 3:27; 1 Thessalonians 4:11, 12; 2 Thessalonians 3:6 12; Titus
3:1.

II. HARD WORK

A. Work Hard

1 Timothy 4:14, 15; 2 Peter 1:10.

B. Diligence

Proverbs 13:4. Lazy people want much but get little, while the diligent
are prospering.

Ruth 3:17, 18; Proverbs 12:27; 13:4; 1 Corinthians 7:20.

C. Examples of Hard Work

Proverbs 6:6–9. Take a lesson from the ants, you lazy fellow. Learn from
their ways and be wise! For though they have no king to make them
work, yet they labor hard all summer, gathering food for the winter.

1 Thessalonians 2:9. Don't you remember, dear brothers, how hard we
worked among you? Night and day we toiled and sweated to earn enough
to live on so that our expenses would not be a burden to anyone there.

Genesis 31:38–42; Ruth 2:7; 1 Chronicles 22:14; Nehemiah 4:6; 4:20, 21;
Proverbs 6:6–11; 1 Corinthians 4:12; 1 Thessalonians 2:9; 2 John 1:8;
Revelation 2:2.

D. Results of Hard Work

Proverbs 12:11. Hard work means prosperity; only a fool idles away his
time.

Proverbs 22:29. Do you know a hard-working man? He shall be
successful and stand before kings!

Proverbs 10:4; 12:11, 14, 24; 13:11; 14:23; 20:13; 22:29; 28:19;
Ecclesiastes 2:10, 24, 25; 3:13, 22; 5:12; 10:17.

E. Hard Work Prerequisite for Pastor

1 Timothy 3:2

F. Balance Your Hard Work

Psalm 127:2. It is senseless for you to work so hard from early morning to late at night, fearing you will starve to death; for God wants his loved ones to get their proper rest.

III. WORK AS UNTO THE LORD

Colossians 3:23, 24. Work hard and cheerfully at all you do, just as though you were working for the Lord and not merely for your masters, remembering that it is the Lord Christ who is going to pay you, giving you your full portion of all he owns. He is the one you are really working for.

Romans 12:11; 2 Corinthians 4:1; Colossians 3:17, 23, 24.

IV. EMPLOYEES ARE REQUIRED TO BE FAITHFUL

A. Faithful Employees

Proverbs 25:13. A faithful employee is as refreshing as a cool day in the hot summertime.

Ephesians 6:5–8. Slaves, obey your masters; be eager to give them your very best. Serve them as you would Christ. Don't work hard only when your master is watching and then shirk when he isn't looking; work hard and with gladness all the time, as though working for Christ, doing the will of God with all your hearts. Remember, the Lord will pay you for each good thing you do, whether you are slave or free.

Proverbs 25:13; Ephesians 6:5–8; Colossians 3:22–25; 1 Timothy 6:1, 2; Titus 2:9, 10; 1 Peter 2:18, 19.

B. Employer Blessed by a Faithful Employee

Genesis 30:27, 29, 30; 39:4, 5; Jeremiah 29:7.

C. The Curse of a Lazy, Unfaithful Employee

Proverbs 10:26. A lazy fellow is a pain to his employers—like smoke in their eyes or vinegar that sets the teeth on edge.

Proverbs 10:26; 14:35; 26:10.

V. EMPLOYERS MUST ALSO BE FAITHFUL

Jeremiah 22:13. And woe to you, King Jehoiakim, for you are building your great palace with forced labor. By not paying wages you are building injustice into its walls and oppression into its doorframes and ceilings.

Leviticus 19:13; Deuteronomy 25:4, 14, 15; Job 31:13–15, 31; Proverbs 27:18; Jeremiah 22:13; Malachi 3:5; Matthew 20:1–16; Ephesians 6:9; Colossians 4:1.

VI. TRAGEDIES OF LAZINESS

Proverbs 18:9. A lazy man is brother to the saboteur.

Proverbs 24:32, 33. Then as I looked, I learned this lesson: "A little extra sleep, a little more slumber, a little folding of the hands to rest" means that poverty will break in upon you suddenly like a robber, and violently like a bandit.

Proverbs 10:4, 5; 15:19; 18:9; 19:15, 24; 20:4; 21:25, 26; 22:13; 23:21; 24:30–32; 26:13; Ecclesiastes 10:18; 1 Thessalonians 5:14; 2 Thessalonians 3:6–12.

ETHICS

I. FOUNDATION OF ETHICS

A. Old Testament

Deuteronomy 5:19–21. You must not steal. You must not tell lies. You must not burn with desire for another man's wife, nor envy him for his home, land, servants, oxen, donkeys, nor anything else he owns.

Proverbs 20:10, 23. The Lord despises every kind of cheating. The Lord loathes all cheating and dishonesty.

Zechariah 8:16, 17. Here is your part: tell the truth. Be fair. Live at peace with everyone. Don't plot to harm others; don't swear that something is true when it isn't! "How I hate all that sort of thing!" says the Lord.

Exodus 20:3–17; 22:3, 6; Deuteronomy 5:16, 19–21; Proverbs 11:1, 3, 5, 6; 12:15; 16:8–11; 19:1; 20:10, 23; 22:28; 31:8, 9; Isaiah 11:1–5; 56:1; 61:8; Ezekiel 45:9–12; Hosea 12:6; Amos 3:10; Zechariah 8:16, 17.

B. New Testament

Romans 13:9, 10. If you love your neighbor as much as you love yourself you will not want to harm or cheat him, or kill him or steal from him. And you won't sin with his wife or want what is his, or do anything else the Ten Commandments say is wrong. All ten are wrapped up in this one, to love your neighbor as you love yourself. Love does no wrong to anyone. That's why it fully satisfies all of God's requirements. It is the only law you need.

Matthew 7:12; Luke 12:15; Romans 13:9, 10.

II. ETHICAL BEHAVIOR

A. Results of Ethical Practices

Proverbs 10:2. Ill-gotten gain brings no lasting happiness; right living does.

Psalm 112:2-9; Proverbs 10:2; 11:18; 28:12; 29:14; Isaiah 33:15.

B. Examples of Good Ethics

1 Kings 9:4; Job 1:8; Jeremiah 22:15-17; 2 Corinthians 7:2.

III. UNETHICAL METHODS

A. Unethical Practices

Deuteronomy 25:16. All who cheat with unjust weights and measurements are detestable to the Lord your God.

Leviticus 19:11, 12; 25:16; 27:17; Psalm 15:5; 62:10, 12; Proverbs 1:10-15; 30:10; Ezekiel 23:25; Hosea 12:7; Amos 2:6-8; Micah 2:1, 2; 6:10-12; 1 Corinthians 6:8.

B. Unethical Behavior Toward the Poor and Underprivileged

Proverbs 22:16, 22, 23. He who gains by oppressing the poor or by bribing the rich shall end in poverty. Don't rob the poor and sick! For the Lord is their defender. If you injure them he will punish you.

Exodus 22:22, 23; 23:6; Deuteronomy 16:19, 20; 25:14, 15; 27:19; Psalm 10:2, 3; Proverbs 11:26; 13:23; 17:5; 22:16, 22, 23; 23:10, 11; 28:8; 29:7; Isaiah 1:16, 17, 23, 24; 3:14; 10:1, 2; Jeremiah 5:26-28; 7:5, 6; Ezekiel 22:6, 7, 29; Amos 4:1-3; 5:10-13; 8:4-6; Zechariah 7:10.

C. Bribes

Exodus 23:8. Take no bribes, for a bribe makes you unaware of what you can clearly see! A bribe hurts the cause of the person who is right.

Exodus 23:8; Deuteronomy 16:19, 20; 27:25; Job 17:5; Psalm 26:9, 10; 58:1, 2; Proverbs 15:27; 17:8, 23; 22:16; 29:4; Ecclesiastes 7:7; Amos 5:12; Micah 3:9-11; 7:3; Habakkuk 1:3, 4; Zechariah 7:8, 9; Matthew 28:12-15.

D. Unethical Judicial Proceedings

Exodus 23:1-3; Leviticus 5:1; 19:15; Deuteronomy 1:17; 2 Chronicles 19:5-11; Proverbs 24:23; Isaiah 5:23.

E. Results of Unethical Practices

Job 27:16-18. The evil man may accumulate money like dust, with closets jammed full of clothing—yes, he may order them made by his tailor, but the innocent shall wear that clothing, and shall divide his silver among them. Every house built by the wicked is as fragile as a spider web, as full of cracks as a leafy booth!

Proverbs 15:27. Dishonest money brings grief to all the family, but hating bribes brings happiness.

Job 27:16-18; Proverbs 11:11; 12:3; 15:27; 20:17, 21; 21:6; 28:2, 28; 29:4; Jeremiah 17:11; Zechariah 5:3, 4.

F. A Man Who Consorts with Prostitutes Will End up in Poverty

Proverbs 5:7-10; 6:25, 26; 9:17, 18.

IV. RELATIVE ETHICS

Judges 17:6. For in those days Israel had no king, so everyone did whatever he wanted to—whatever seemed right in his own eyes.

V. ETHICAL AND UNETHICAL MAN CONTRASTED

Proverbs 12:12, 13, 17; 14:5.

VI. RESTITUTION

Leviticus 6:1–5; 25:17, 18; Numbers 5:7; Proverbs 6:30, 31; Ezekiel 33:14, 15; Luke 19:8, 9.

INVESTING

I. SAVING

A. Admonition to Save

Proverbs 21:20. The wise man saves for the future, but the foolish man spends whatever he gets.

Proverbs 21:17, 20, 21; 30:24, 25.

B. Why Save?

Proverbs 22:3. A prudent man foresees the difficulties ahead and prepares for them; the simpleton goes blindly on and suffers the consequences.

II. INVESTING

A. Investing Is Acceptable

Matthew 25:14–29; Luke 19:12–24.

B. Systematic Investing

Proverbs 21:5. Steady plodding brings prosperity; hasty speculation brings poverty.

C. Develop Your Business

Proverbs 24:3, 4. Any enterprise is built by wise planning, becomes strong through common sense, and profits wonderfully by keeping abreast of the facts.

Proverbs 24:27. Develop your business first before building your house.

III. AVOID RISKY INVESTMENTS AND GET-RICH-QUICK SCHEMES

Proverbs 28:22. Trying to get rich quick is evil and leads to poverty.

Ecclesiastes 5:13–15. There is another serious problem I have seen everywhere—savings are put into risky investments that turn sour, and soon there is nothing left to pass on to one's son. The man who speculates is soon back to where he began—with nothing. This, as I said, is a very serious problem, for all his hard work has been for nothing; he has been working for the wind. It is all swept away.

Proverbs 13:11; 21:5; 28:20, 22; Ecclesiastes 5:13–15.

IV. INHERITANCE

Proverbs 13:22. When a good man dies, he leaves an inheritance to his grandchildren; but when the sinner dies, his wealth is stored up for the godly.

Genesis 24:36; 25:5; Numbers 27:8–11; Proverbs 13:22.

V. LENDING

A. Old Testament Principles

   1) loans were to be interest free to fellow-Jews

Exodus 22:25. If you lend money to a needy fellow-Hebrew, you are not to handle the transaction in an ordinary way, with interest.

Exodus 22:25; Leviticus 25:35–37.

   2) interest could be charged to foreigners

Deuteronomy 23:19, 20.

   3) a lender could not hold security which was essential to the well-being of the borrower

Deuteronomy 24:17. Justice must be given to migrants and orphans and you must never accept a widow's garment in pledge of her debt.

Exodus 22:26, 27; Deuteronomy 24:10–13, 17; Ezekiel 18:5, 7–9.

   4) forgiveness of debts

Deuteronomy 15:1, 2; Nehemiah 10:31.

   5) loans were to be made on the basis of needs irrespective of risk

Deuteronomy 15:7–9.

B. New Testament Principles of Lending

   1) the principle of lending was broadened by the New Testament to include all people with repayment not expected

Luke 6:34, 35. And if you lend money to those who can repay you, what good is that? Even the most wicked will lend to their own kind for full return! Love your enemies! Do good to them! And don't be concerned about the fact that they won't repay.

2) do we give or do we lend?

Matthew 5:42 (NASB). Give to him who asks of you, and do not turn away from him who wants to borrow from you.

3) loan repayment is incumbent upon the borrower before God

Psalm 37:21. Evil men borrow and "cannot pay it back"! But the good man returns what he owes with some extra besides.

C. Charging Interest on Investments Is Proper

Luke 19:23. Then why didn't you deposit the money in the bank so that I could at least get interest on it?

SHARING

I. SHARING IS AN HISTORICAL PRACTICE

Genesis 14:20. Then Abram gave Melchizedek a tenth of all the spoils.

Genesis 4:3, 5; 8:20, 21; 14:20; 28:20–22; 1 Chronicles 29:3–8; 2 Chronicles 24:6, 9, 11, 12; Proverbs 10:16; Isaiah 32:7, 8; Haggai 1:3–6, 9–11; Matthew 10:8; Luke 11:39–41; Acts 10:1–4, 31; Romans 12:1, 8; James 2:14–16; 1 John 3:17, 18.

II. THE PURPOSE OF SHARING IS TO BENEFIT THE GIVER

A. It Is More Blessed to Give Than to Receive

Luke 6:38. For if you give, you will get! Your gift will return to you in full and overflowing measure, pressed down, shaken together to make room for more, and running over. Whatever measure you use to give—large or small—will be used to measure what is given back to you.

Acts 20:35. It is more blessed to give than to receive.

1 Chronicles 29:9; Ezra 6:15–17, 22; Nehemiah 12:43; Proverbs 11:24, 25; 19:6; Luke 6:38; Acts 20:35; 2 Corinthians 9:6–14; Philippians 4:19.

B. To Teach Us to Remember God Should Be First in Our Lives

Deuteronomy 14:23. The purpose of tithing is to teach you always to put God first in your lives.

Deuteronomy 14:23; 26:2, 3, 10; 1 Chronicles 29:14.

C. God Does Not Need Our Gifts

Psalm 50:10–12. For all the animals of field and forest are mine! The cattle on a thousand hills! And all the birds upon the mountains! If I were hungry, I would not mention it to you—for all the world is mine, and everything in it.

Psalm 50:10–12; Acts 17:24, 25.

D. Giving Is an Eternal Investment

1 Timothy 6:18, 19. Tell them to use their money to do good. They should be rich in good works and should give happily to those in need, always being ready to share with others whatever God has given them. By doing this they will be storing up treasures for themselves in heaven—it is the only safe investment for eternity!

Matthew 6:19–21; Luke 12:21, 32–34; 1 Timothy 6:18, 19; Revelation 2:9.

  1) we can take nothing with us when we die

Job 1:21. "I came naked from my mother's womb," he said, "and I shall have nothing when I die. The Lord gave me everything I had, and they were his to take away. Blessed be the name of the Lord."

Job 1:21; James 1:10, 11.

III. HOW MUCH SHOULD WE SHARE?

A. Tithe

  1) pre-Mosaic law

Genesis 28:22. And I [Jacob] will give you back a tenth of everything you give me!

Genesis 14:20; 28:22.

  2) Old Testament law

Malachi 3:8–10. You have robbed me of the tithes and offerings due me. And so the awesome curse of God is cursing you, for your whole nation has been robbing me. Bring all the tithes into the storehouse so that there will be food enough in my Temple; if you do, I will open up the windows of heaven for you and pour out a blessing so great you won't have room enough to take it in!

Exodus 22:29; Leviticus 27:30–32; Numbers 18:21–30; Deuteronomy 14:22, 23, 27–29; 26:12, 13; 2 Chronicles 31:4–10; Nehemiah 10:35–39; Malachi 3:8–10.

  3) New Testament references to tithing

Matthew 23:23–25; Luke 11:42; 18:12; Hebrews 7:1–10.

B. Offering

Deuteronomy 16:10. At that time to him a free-will offering
proportionate in size to his blessing upon you as judged by the amount of
your harvest.

Genesis 4:4; Exodus 25:1–7; 35:4–9, 20–22, 29; Deuteronomy 16:10, 17;
Ezra 2:68, 69; 1 Corinthians 16:2; 2 Corinthians 8:11, 12; 9:11.

C. Proportionate Sharing

1 Corinthians 16:2. On the Lord's Day each of you should put aside
something from what you have earned during the week, and use it for
this offering. The amount depends on how much the Lord has helped you
earn.

Deuteronomy 15:14; 16:9, 10, 16, 17; 2 Corinthians 8:10–12; 9:5–11.

D. Sacrificial Giving

2 Corinthians 8:3. They gave not only what they could afford, but far
more; and I can testify that they did it because they wanted to, and not
because of nagging on my part.

2 Samuel 24:22–24; 1 Chronicles 22—24; 29:3–5; Ezra 2:68, 69; Mark
12:41–44; Luke 21:1–4; 2 Corinthians 8:1–4, 9; 11:7–12; 12:13, 14.

E. Attitude Is More Important Than Amount

Hosea 6:6. I don't want your sacrifices—I want your love; I don't want
your offerings—I want you to know me.

1 Samuel 15:22; Psalm 40:6; 52:7–9; Proverbs 21:3, 27; Isaiah 1:11–13;
Jeremiah 7:21–23; Hosea 6:6; Micah 6:6–8; Haggai 2:14; Matthew 6:1–4;
9:13; 12:7; 23:23–25; Luke 11:42; Hebrews 11:4.

   1) cheerful giving, the desired attitude

2 Corinthians 9:7. Everyone must make up his own mind as to how much
he should give. Don't force anyone to give more than he really wants to,
for cheerful givers are the ones God prizes.

2 Corinthians 8:7, 8; 9:7.

   2) the wrong attitude

2 Corinthians 9:3–5.

F. The Pattern of Sharing

1 Corinthians 16:2. On every Lord's Day each of you should put aside
something from what you have earned during the week, and use it for
this offering. The amount depends on how much the Lord has helped you
earn. Don't wait until I get there and try to collect it all at once.

IV. WHOM DO WE SHARE WITH?

Ecclesiastes 11:1, 2. Give generously, for your gifts will return to you
later. Divide your gifts among many, for in the days ahead you yourself
may need much help.

A. Family and Relatives

1 Timothy 5:8. But anyone who won't care for his own relatives when they need help, especially those living in his own family, has no right to say he is a Christian. Such a person is worse than the heathen.

Leviticus 25:35; Matthew 15:4–6; Mark 7:10, 11; 1 Timothy 5:8, 16.

B. Christian Work and Workers

1 Timothy 5:17, 18. Pastors who do their work well should be paid well and should be highly appreciated, especially those who work hard at both preaching and teaching. For the Scriptures say, "Never tie up the mouth of an ox when it is treading out the grain—let him eat as he goes along!" And in another place, "Those who work deserve their pay!"
Deuteronomy 18:1–5; 2 Chronicles 31:18, 19; Nehemiah 12:44; Isaiah 23:18; Matthew 10:8–10; Mark 6:8, 9; Luke 8:3; 9:3, 4; 10:4–7; 1 Corinthians 9:4–15, 18, 19; 2 Corinthians 11:7–9; 12:13, 14; Galatians 6:6; Philippians 4:10, 14–19; 1 Timothy 5:17, 18; Titus 3:13, 14; 3 John 1:5–8.

C. The Poor

Proverbs 28:27. If you give to the poor, your needs will be supplied! But a curse upon those who close their eyes to poverty.

Exodus 23:11; Leviticus 19:9, 10; Nehemiah 8:10; Job 29:12–15; Psalm 9:18; 41:1–3; Proverbs 14:21, 31; 19:17; 21:13; 22:9; 28:27; Isaiah 58:6, 7, 10, 11; Ezekiel 16:49; Daniel 4:27; Luke 3:11; 10:33–35; 14:12–14; 16:19–31; 19:8, 9; Acts 9:36; 20:33–35; 1 Corinthians 11:20–22; Galatians 2:10; Ephesians 4:28; Hebrews 13:16; 1 Peter 4:9; Revelation 2:19.

D. Christians in Need

Romans 12:13. When God's children are in need, you be the one to help them out. And get in the habit of inviting guests home for dinner or, if they need lodging, for the night.

Acts 2:44–46; 4:32–37; 11:27–30; Romans 12:13; 15:25–28, 31; 2 Corinthians 8:10–15; 9:1, 2; Galatians 6:10.

E. Widows

1 Timothy 5:3–7

V. GIFTS AND SACRIFICES FROM THE LORD

Ephesians 4:8. When Christ returned triumphantly to heaven after his resurrection and victory over Satan, he gave generous gifts to men.

Ephesians 4:8; Hebrews 9:14; 1 Peter 1:4, 18.

VI. PUT FAITHFUL MEN IN CHARGE OF MONEY

1 Corinthians 16:3, 4. When I come I will send your loving gift with a letter to Jerusalem, to be taken there by trustworthy messengers you

yourself will choose. And if it seems wise for me to go along too, then we can travel together.

Nehemiah 13:13; Acts 1:1–6; 11:27–30; 1 Corinthians 16:3, 4; 2 Corinthians 8:16–21.

VII. FALSE TEACHERS ARE OFTEN AFTER MONEY

1 Timothy 6:5. These arguers—their minds warped by sin—don't know how to tell the truth; to them the Good News is just a means of making money. Keep away from them.

Zephaniah 3:4; Mark 11:15–17; 12:40; Luke 19:45, 46; John 2:14–16; 1 Thessalonians 2:5; 1 Timothy 6:5; 2 Peter 2:3, 14, 15; Jude 1:11.

BUDGET

I. A BUDGET HELPS PLANNING AHEAD

Proverbs 14:8. The wise man looks ahead. The fool attempts to fool himself and won't face facts.

Luke 14:28–30. But don't begin until you count the cost. For who would begin construction of a building without first getting estimates and then checking to see if he has enough money to pay the bills?

II. A BUDGET HELPS YOU KEEP ABREAST OF THE FACTS

Proverbs 24:3, 4. Any enterprise is built by wise planning, becomes strong through common sense, and profits wonderfully by keeping abreast of the facts.

Proverbs 27:23–27. Riches can disappear fast. And the king's crown doesn't stay in his family forever—so watch your business interests closely. Know the state of your flocks and your herds; then there will be lamb's wool enough for clothing, and goat's milk enough for food for all your household after the hay is harvested, and the new crop appears, and the mountain grasses are gathered in.

III. A BUDGET HELPS YOU STAY ORGANIZED

1 Corinthians 14:33. God is not one who likes things to be disorderly and upset.

WEALTH

I. PERSPECTIVE OF WEALTH

A. Proper Perspective of Wealth

Jeremiah 9:23, 24; John 6:27; James 1:9–11.

B. Eternal Perspective of Wealth

Proverbs 11:4. Your riches won't help you on Judgment Day; only righteousness counts then.

1 Corinthians 7:30, 31. Happiness or sadness or wealth should not keep anyone from doing God's work. Those in frequent contact with the exciting things the world offers should make good use of their opportunities without stopping to enjoy them; for the world in its present form will soon be gone.

Proverbs 11:4, 18; Ezekiel 7:10, 11, 19; Luke 18:28–30; 1 Corinthians 7:30, 31; 1 Timothy 6:7; Hebrews 10:34; 11:24, 25.

C. How Wealth Relates to Happiness

Ecclesiastes 5:10, 11. He who loves money shall never have enough. The foolishness of thinking that wealth brings happiness! The more you have the more you spend, right up to the limits of your income, so what is the advantage of wealth—except perhaps to watch it as it runs through your fingers!

Luke 12:15. Beware! Don't always be wishing for what you don't have. For real life and real living are not related to how rich we are.

Proverbs 13:7; Ecclesiastes 5:10, 11; Luke 12:13–20; 2 Corinthians 6:10; 1 Timothy 6:6, 7.

D. Things More Valuable Than Wealth

Matthew 16:26. What profit is there if you gain the whole world—and lose eternal life? What can be compared with the value of eternal life?

1 Peter 1:7. Your faith is far more precious to God than mere gold.

Job 28:17–19; Psalm 49:6–9; 119:71, 72; Proverbs 3:13–15; 8:8–11, 18–21; 10:22; 11:16; 15:16; 16:16, 19; 20:15; 22:1; 28:6; Ecclesiastes 7:1, 11, 12; Matthew 16:26; Mark 8:36; Luke 9:25; 1 Peter 1:7, 18.

E. The Futility of Wealth

Proverbs 11:28. Trust in your money and down you go! Trust in God and flourish as a tree!

Psalm 39:5, 6; Proverbs 11:28; Ecclesiastes 4:7, 8.

F. Balance of Wealth

Proverbs 30:7–9. O God, I beg two favors from you before I die: First,

help me never to tell a lie. Second, give me neither poverty nor riches!
Give me just enough to satisfy my needs! For if I grow rich, I may
become content without God. And if I am too poor, I may steal, and thus
insult God's holy name.

II. DANGER OF WEALTH

A. Trusting in Wealth

Proverbs 18:11. The rich man thinks of his wealth as an impregnable
defense, a high wall of safety. What a dreamer!

Job 31:24-28; Proverbs 11:28; 18:11, 23; 28:11; Jeremiah 48:7; 49:4-6.
31, 32; Ezekiel 28:2-5; Matthew 13:22; 19:16-24; Mark 4:18, 19;
10:20-30; Luke 8:14; 18:18-27; Romans 2:22; 1 Corinthians 7:30-31;
Colossians 3:5; 1 Timothy 6:9, 10, 17; 1 John 2:15-17; Revelation 3:17,
18.

B. Danger of Greed, Covetousness, and Loving Money

Ephesians 5:5. You can be sure of this: The kingdom of Christ and of God
will never belong to anyone who is impure or greedy, for a greedy person
is really an idol worshiper.

1 Timothy 6:9, 10. But people who long to be rich soon begin to do all
kinds of wrong things to get money, things that hurt them and make
them evil minded and finally send them to hell itself. For the love of
money is the first step toward all kinds of sin.

1 Samuel 7:2, 3; Psalm 37:1-3; Proverbs 23:1; 28:25; Ecclesiastes 4:4;
Ezekiel 7:19, 20; Habakkuk 2:5; Mark 7:20-22; Acts 8:18-20; Romans
1:28, 29; 1 Corinthians 5:11; 6:10; Ephesians 5:3, 5; 2 Timothy 3:2; James
3:16; 4:1-3.

C. Evil Deeds Done for Wealth

Matthew 26:14, 15. Then Judas Iscariot, one of the twelve apostles, went
to the chief priests, and asked, "How much will you pay me to get Jesus
into your hands?" And they gave him thirty silver coins.

Judges 16:5, 17-19; Esther 3:8-11, 13; Obadiah 1:13; Matthew 26: 14,
15; 27:5-10; Acts 1:18; 16:16-19.

D. Wealth Used to Worship Idols

Hosea 10:1; Habakkuk 1:16; Acts 19:24-26.

E. Wealth That Leads to Rich and Prideful Men

Ezekiel 7:10, 11; Luke 6:24, 25.

III. GOD'S PEOPLE AND WEALTH

A. God's People Who Were Wealthy

2 Chronicles 9:13, 14. Solomon received a billion dollars worth of gold
each year from the kings of Arabia and many other lands that paid

annual tribute to him. In addition, there was a trade balance from the exports of his merchants.

Genesis 13:1, 2, 5; 26:13, 14; 30:43; 31:9; Ruth 2:1; 2 Chronicles 9:13, 14; 32:28, 29; Job 1:10; Daniel 6:28.

B. God's People Who Were Poor

1 Corinthians 1:26; 2 Corinthians 11:27.

C. Church Leaders Should Not Love Money

1 Timothy 3:1–3; Titus 1:7.

D. Don't Favor the Rich

James 2:1–9.

E. Kingdom of God for the Poor

Luke 6:20, 21; 7:22.

IV. ADVANTAGES AND DISADVANTAGES OF WEALTH

A. Advantages of Wealth

Proverbs 10:15; 14:20; 19:4; Ecclesiastes 5:18–20.

B. Disadvantages of Wealth

Proverbs 13:8; 14:20; 19:7; Ecclesiastes 5:12.

V. WEALTH IS FLEETING

Ecclesiastes 7:14. Enjoy prosperity whenever you can, and when hard times strike, realize that God gives one as well as the other—so that everyone will realize that nothing is certain in this life.

Ecclesiastes 7:14; Ezekiel 27:32–36; 28:12–17; 31:8–11, 14; Micah 6:14; Zephaniah 1:11–13, 18; 2:15; Zechariah 11:3–5; Revelation 18:11–19.

VI. QUESTION OF THE PROSPERITY OF THE WICKED

Proverbs 24:19, 20. Don't envy the wicked. Don't covet his riches. For the evil man has no future; his light will be snuffed out.

Psalm 17:13–15; 37:7; 49:10–17; 52:7; 73:1–20; Proverbs 24:19, 20; Ecclesiastes 8:14; Jeremiah 12:1–3; Habakkuk 2:9, 12, 13; Revelation 18:3.

HERITAGE

Psalm 112:1, 2. Praise the Lord! For all who fear God and trust in him are blessed beyond expression. Yes, happy is the man who delights in doing his commands. His children shall be honored everywhere, for good men's sons have a special heritage.

Proverbs 20:7. It is a wonderful heritage to have an honest father.

Proverbs 22:6. Teach a child to choose the right path, and when he is older he will remain upon it.

CONTENTMENT

I. CONTENTMENT CAN BE LEARNED

Philippians 4:11–13. Not that I was ever in need, for I have learned how to get along happily whether I have much or little. I know how to live on almost nothing or with everything. I have learned the secret of contentment in every situation, whether it be a full stomach or hunger, plenty or want; for I can do everything God asks me to with the help of Christ who gives me the strength and power.

II. BE CONTENT WITH WHAT YOU HAVE

Hebrews 13:5 (NASB). Let your way of life be free from the love of money, being content with what you have; for He Himself has said, "I will never desert you, nor will I ever forsake you."

III. BE CONTENT WITH FOOD AND CLOTHING

1 Timothy 6:8 (NASB). And if we have food and covering, with these we shall be content.

IV. CONTENTMENT NOT IN WEALTH

Psalm 17:15. But as for me, my contentment is not in wealth but in seeing you and knowing all is well between us. And when I awake in heaven, I will be fully satisfied, for I will see you face to face.

V. BE CONTENT WITH YOUR WAGE

Luke 3:14. "And us," asked some of the soldiers, "what about us?" John [the Baptist] replied, "Don't extort money by threats and violence; don't accuse anyone of what you know he didn't do; and be content with your pay!"

VI. GODLINESS IS A MEANS OF GAIN WHEN ACCOMPANIED BY CONTENTMENT

1 Timothy 6:6 (NASB). But godliness actually is a means of great gain, when accompanied by contentment.

QUESTIONS AND ANSWERS

I. SHOULD WOMEN WORK?

Psalm 128:3. Your wife shall be contented in your home. And look at all those children! There they sit around the dinner table as vigorous and healthy as young olive trees.

Proverbs 31:13–17. She finds wool and flax and busily spins it. She buys imported foods, brought by ship from distant ports. She gets up before dawn to prepare breakfast for her household, and plans the day's work for her servant girls. She goes out to inspect a field and buys it; with her own hands she plants a vineyard. She is energetic, a hard worker, and watches for bargains.

Psalm 128:3, 4; Proverbs 31:13–29; Titus 2:4.

II. SHOULD THE CHRISTIAN PAY TAXES?

Romans 13:5–7. Obey the laws, then, for two reasons: first, to keep from being punished, and second, just because you know you should. Pay your taxes too, for these same two reasons. For government workers need to be paid so they can keep on doing God's work, serving you. Pay everyone whatever he ought to have: pay your taxes and import duties gladly . . . .

Matthew 17:24–27; 22:17–21; Mark 12:14–17; Luke 20:22–25; Romans 13:5–7.

III. SHOULD WE EXPECT TO PROSPER?

3 John 1:2 (TEV) Dear friend, I am praying that you prosper in all as your soul prospers.

NOTES

1. Charles L. Allen, *God's Psychiatry* (Old Tappan, NJ: Revell, 1953).
2. David McConaughy, *Money, the Acid Test* (Philadelphia: Westminster Press, 1918), pp. 24, 25.
3. Richard Halverson, *Perspective* (Los Angeles: Cowman Publications, 1957), p. 59.
4. Jim Ferri, "Is Rich a State of Mind?," *TWA Ambassador* (St. Paul, MN: 1978), p. 58.
5. Carol Pine, "Getting a Charge Out of Youth," *Business Today* (Princeton: 1978), p. 22.
6. George Fooshee, *You Can Be Financially Free* (Old Tappan, NJ: Revell, 1976), p. 26.
7. *Ibid.*, pp. 78–80.
8. Herb Goldberg and Robert Lewis, *Money Madness* (New York: Morrow, 1978), pp. 13, 14.
9. John Haggai, *New Hope for Planet Earth* (Nashville: Thomas Nelson, 1974), p. 36.
10. Francis Schaeffer, *No Little People* (Downers Grove, IL: InterVarsity Press, 1974).
11. Roger Palms, "I'm Not Hungry," *Decision* (Billy Graham Evangelical Association, 1978).
12. Op. cit., Halverson, p. 27.
13. Leslie B. Flynn, *Your God and Your Gold* (Grand Rapids: Zondervan), p. 112.

14. Haddon Robinson, "Testimony of a Checkbook," *Christian Medical Society Journal* (1976), p. 3.
15. Jerry and Mary White, *Your Job—Survival or Satisfaction?* (Grand Rapids: Zondervan, 1977), p. 74.
16. Mark Hatfield, "Excellence, the Christian Standard," *Collegiate Challenge Magazine* (May, 1965).
17. *Op. cit.,* Schaeffer.
18. Maxine Hancock, *Living on Less and Liking It More* (Chicago: Moody Press, 1976), pp. 43, 44.